Academic Revolution

Life Through the Seams of Jeans Series

By

Justin Louis-Jean

&

Pierce Mortensen

First Published September 2022.
Revised Edition July 2023.

ISBN
Library and Archives Canada
Paperback 978-1-7390277-6-6
Hardcover 978-1-7390277-7-3

Cover design by Kabrena L. Robinson
Published in Canada by Eva-Michelle & Family Publishing
www.evamichelleandfamily.com

Table of Contents

Problem 7

The Inevitable. The Unexpected.

Introduction

I don't know about you, but schools are not what they should be. Instead of preparing students for the future, they focus on the past and are slow to evolve with the world around them. They keep their conservative values which hold everyone back with them. We can see it in everything they do, how they treat their students like clones, and place them in desks that are in columns and rows. They don't respect how students learn, or their basic needs like food or simply using the bathroom. The best schools are determined by performance, but performance is completely based on the grades from tests, and exams that only measure how much information you can retain and spit back out.

The school system needs to find an innovative way to instruct students if it wants to keep up with the modern age. The people in charge have not been in school for a long time and spend more time focusing on the small things than looking at the big picture. The reality is, the solution needs to come from the mind of a student, someone who has gone through school, and seen where the problems lie firsthand. Over the course of seven chapters, this book will highlight the most vital problems with our school system and show the best path to solve them in a constructive way. The goal of this book is to "educate about education", for both the student and the teacher, and hopefully make life in school a little easier for everyone involved.

Problem 1

Old Age Values

How, many times have you looked at the clock and know that it is a few minutes until class is over but then your teacher says, "The bell doesn't dismiss you, I do." We wait in front of the door, looking at the clock that's already passed the time, yet we don't dare leave the room until we hear that bell ring. Our "student brains" have been conditioned by that specific ring to tell us when we should be in or out of class, and if you've ever been to school one day where those bells are uncoordinated, you can see how it makes everyone just a little crazy. Does the name Ivan Pavlov ring a bell?

Most schooling systems are based upon mass productivity and mass control (controlling who comes in and out, when and what we eat, and oftentimes even what we think!). They give us tests based on memorization instead of comprehension, which are the learning methods for teaching factory workers, not individuals. This isn't the way things are across the globe, however. If you take Finland for example, their education system was at the bottom of the food chain in the 1960s, but they decided to massively reform their schooling by going against the grain of the classic system. They decided to adopt innovative ideas like removing homework from the curriculum and reducing school hours to twenty hours a week over four days! They even push their children to be independent at young ages. This is not a system that bases its education on a factory's profits, but one that sees the individual as the world of the future[1].

Another big attribute of factory workers is their ability to follow instructions. The reason students depend on their grades to pass their classes is the same reason why factory workers' success depends on following instructions. The problem with that is in today's world we need people who can do the opposite of what factory workers are supposed to do and that's creativity, communication about their ideas and

---

[1] YouTube, Visions of Helsinki, Why Finland has the best education system in the world. September 15th, 2016.

collaboration with others. According to psychoanalysis Jean Piaget, a child's cognitive process is fundamentally different from those of an adult because children move through four stages of development independently. Because of that, a teacher must provide tasks that are appropriate to the child's stage of development and nurture independent thinking and creativity.

"The goal of education is to create men and women who are capable of doing new things. Not simply repeating what other generations have done, men and women who are innovative, creative and discoverers. The second goal of education is to form minds which could be critical and verify not just accept everything that's offered" [2]

There's also a growing discussion about how schools don't properly teach students life skills they will need as adults. There are no classes in high school that discuss the essential topics: money management, taxes, building credit, or even simply applying for a job. As students, we barely understand how society runs, what kind of jobs will exist or how the subjects we learn could be practical for us in the future. This is why when we learn about mitochondria in cells or the Pythagorean theorem, we feel like these lessons are useless. They do not have any obvious applications in the day-to-day life of most people. I'm not saying these classes shouldn't be available, but why waste students' time by

[2] *TOP 25 QUOTES BY JEAN PIAGET (of 73) | A-Z Quotes*. A-Z Quotes. August 11th, 2022.

forcing them to take those classes when there are more useful things to understand. This is why many students lose interest in school in the later years because they start to encounter needless hard classes that have no practical use. These classes become filters for students who can keep up with these courses, while it punishes those who aren't as skilled in math and science.

The system is even set up in a way that teachers are forced to push students to get good marks in these classes too, so that even if they recognize how pointless these classes are, they have to be good in them. The thing is, if you don't understand the subject, the teachers are not there to help you. We can't raise our hand if we don't understand or we are blamed for not listening, we can't get help from classmates or we are blamed for slowing down the class, and yet we get blamed for not participating when we don't know what's going on. The problem doesn't stop in school though, even at home we see parents reinforcing the rigid grading system by pushing their kids to do well in it. For many parents, failing grades are a symbol of failure for their children, and they blame them for not doing well without understanding their children's perspective. Parents need to understand that failure is simply your **First Attempt In Learning** and that it is something that should be appreciated instead of punished, especially when their child is putting in the effort. The school system is made to have students fail, that's why the bell curve was invented, and it's what keeps many people from succeeding. In fact, it's the polygamy effect[3], students across the globe face every day. When many students fail, they lose all their confidence, not because they can't succeed but because they are in a system that has convinced them that they can't. Any student can succeed if you give them the chance to do so, but this idea goes against the grading system that exists today, so schools try to ignore this as a possibility.

There are two types of mindsets for every disappointment you will ever face, the fixed mindset is when you tell yourself that your worth is the grade on the paper, it's degrading, isn't it? (pun intended). But that's how it is, the grading system is fixed and when you reach a hundred percent or A+ it's considered that you've memorized everything and there's nothing left. But since you're your worst critic, you feel as if you could have done better. Instead, the growth mindset where you tell yourself that there's always room for improvement should be practised. When it comes to grades, you should approach it with a growth mindset and look at your mistakes from an optimist

---

[3] Perera, A., & McLeod, S. The Pygmalion Effect. Simplysociology.com. April 6th, 2022.

point of view, you're able to improve. And since there will be more than one test and even if you fail some tests that doesn't mean you can't bounce back on the next. However, teachers if you want your students to bounce back, you need to give them the opportunity. For example, the first thing you do on the day after a test you take the next class to correct the exam together to show the students their mistakes. So, they could practise laying out the bricks and use them as steps as opposed to carrying their mistakes until they get home. And I say to get home because when it came to me and my tests, my parents would always ask me about the outcome of a test I had that day and if I made mistakes, they would ask me what I could do to improve, but I don't have the answer as to what I got wrong, how could I improve on my next test?

Another aspect that makes Finland different is the fact that they don't have exams since they prioritize understanding a subject versus just learning it. They also have the funding for the teachers to run the extra race and that is that they have no private schools since they believe that education shouldn't cost money and it makes sure that no kids are seen as 'rich' or 'poor' since they go to the same school. The Ministry of Education in Finland quotes *"All the schools in Finland are equal since it's illegal in Finland to set up a school and charge tuition and that's why private schools don't exist. Meaning that the rich parents have to make sure that the public schools are great by making the rich kids go to school with everybody else. Resulting in those having to go to school with everyone else and having those other kids as friends; meaning that when those rich kids grow older, they'll think twice before screwing them over "*[4]. Imagine what we can do if we'd apply that logic to boy-only schools, girl-only schools or what about having everyone grow up in the same learning environment and think about classism, racism, and sexism? More on that in my other books.

School teaches us how to memorize dots, like information but true education should teach you how to connect those dots, like pieces of a puzzle. Think of the game of *Connect the Dots* and there's a hidden picture but you won't know what it is until you connect them all. You see if you memorize where the dots are without tracing them in order, you won't know what your potential and you won't understand the bigger picture. However, if we knew how to connect those dots, we'd be able to see the big picture and since everyone has a different picture, then it's up to them to trace their path. Also, you have to go through many jobs to find and fund your career. Even if that takes a long time and you feel like you may as well stick to your current job because you are safe and it gives you income, but you're not happy. Then it doesn't matter how many jobs you have or had. As long as you don't forget the gift you have since it takes many of those to shape you into what you want to be.

---

[4] YouTube, ABC News Australia, "Why Finland's schools outperform most others across the developed world" January 31st, 2020.

Schools vs. Jobs

There are only a couple of things that school itself has taught us and no, it's not the curriculum it's how the school system is designed. It was made to reflect work and the long days are one of the ways that school affects your mental health. It taught us that at work we have long and tiring days that we should expect to be constantly supervised and that your peers or co-workers aren't always your friends, and they're often there to compete for high grades or a promotion. It shows us that if we don't care about ourselves, no one will, and that school reflects a "professional" environment. As in, you have to show up on time or else there are consequences, you have deadlines to achieve something, and your supervisor doesn't care for your excuses for not making it since they have their stuff to deal with. If you think school and work are the same deal, you get the same hours.

For example, you go to school five days a week, for six hours a day, to complete thirty hours of a school week; minus five hours of lunch breaks over the course of the week, so as a student, you do twenty-five hours of class. Compared to a full-time job, it's eight hours, five days a week, for forty hours in total, minus two and a half hours of lunch break; so, you're left with thirty-seven and a half hours of full work throughout the week. You legally cannot operate on yourself or anyone close to you since emotions can come into play and affect your professionalism or performance. This means that, unlike school, your work life, and home life are designed to be two separate things. As a social worker myself, it's illegal for me to bring my patients' documents home for confidential reasons. Therefore, I must either stay and complete them after working hours, or finish them first thing in the morning, so I never bring my work at home.

"School violates labour hours because of homework," as in why are students expected to do more work than a full-time job? For part-time, just like any job, you can either apply to go as a full or part-time student in college or university.

According to CIEB[5] (Center on International Education Benchmarking) students from the first grade in Finland get twenty fixed hours of school a week, without counting the lunch period. Students get so much homework they're less in touch with their friends because they both have work to do, and this lack of time with friends can affect our mental health over time. Well according to the World Innovation Summit for Education (WISE) on YouTube, and their video on homework, Finland does it better[6] their students were divided into two groups and both groups were learning a different subject in a day. According to them, it helps with individual learning and the teacher can understand what is going on in the student's heads and then the student can

---

[5] CIEB, "How Long Is The Average School Day". http://ncee.org/wp-content/uploads/2018/02/SchoolYearStatv5.pdf
[6] YouTube, World Innovation Summit for Education (WISE), "homework: Finland dose it better" October 25th, 2013.

benefit from some one-on-one time with the teacher to identify any learning difficulties.

"The philosophy is that all learning should happen inside the school and daily homework should not exceed thirty minutes. One important thing is motivation, if the workload is not overwhelming then it's fun, and too much repetitive work will discourage them."

- Ville Teittinen, Teacher.

Also, there is the fact that since homework is minimal and if you're able to finish quickly you can enjoy the rest of your evening.

My concern isn't only with the amount of homework that you get in school, it's also that a lot of teachers teach things that have nothing to do with the homework you're assigned and then expect you to complete it at home even when you don't know what you're doing. Teachers want their students to fully comprehend something through homework, but there are those students who have other things to do when they get home (like me). Once they get home, their brains automatically switch from school to home mode, by the time they look at their homework, their brains are fried and they end up just staring at it (also like me in math, science, history, etc.) Teachers should also give time for students to do their homework in class and go over it to make sure everyone understands. This would increase participation and understanding, and it would even be time efficient to help struggling students. Because let's be honest learning isn't hard, you just need to find a way of learning you like and if no one is there to help you, that's when you self-educate. The problem is that most of the time we have too many things to learn between all the required and "mandatory optional" classes needed to get your diploma. What will determine if you have an easy or hard year is the length of your class, multiplied by their load to the power of the number of classes you have.

When I was in the seventh grade, I would use my recess or independent work time to complete my homework so then I didn't have any when I got home, sounds smart right? But often teachers would come to me and say: *"Justin, it's not the time to do this. You'll have time when you get home but right now, we are doing X or Y."* What the teacher failed to realize was that the reason I'd be doing other things is because chances are, I'm done doing what the teacher told me to do so I'd be off completing something else. I don't see a problem with this; if I'm not doing anything interesting, and the teacher isn't teaching, then it makes sense that I should use my time effectively in class to complete my work, so it doesn't have such a big effect on my life outside of school.

Teachers, how do you want your students to be ahead of everyone if you stop them from advancing in their way? I'm trying to understand who you are talking to when you say *"Class, we're behind schedule."*

Since we all know that you can't compare two children; as a teacher, you should also know that your students learn

11

at different speeds, so comparing them to another class is just unfair. You'll often have multiple teachers teaching the same subject, so you can always ask them what they did to get ahead. We all know that teaching is a two-person job between the student and the teacher; the teacher can't do their job without the student, and vice versa since independent learning works until you think you've learned everything. What teachers and employers forget is that their employees and students have their own lives as well. So, if your class is performing horribly, look in the mirror and ask yourself if it is you who doesn't understand the subject well enough to teach it, rather than them being unable to understand it. It's also good to think about if you're giving too many tasks to do in too little time. You want your students to succeed right?

Imagine these two scenarios: you go home from a long day at school and your parents say, *"I received a call from the principal's office and your grades are terrible, how could you let things get this bad?"* In this response, you're lacking empathy towards your child because you are dismissing the problem that they have, and since you're being dismissive, they're not going to talk about why they got the low grades in the first place. Since the problem isn't addressed, they won't get over what's troubling them, and now they're worst off because you're dismissing them as well. Consider this, you come home from a long day at school and your parents tell you *"I received a call from the principal's office, and your grades aren't looking too good.*

Are you doing, okay? Is there something you want to discuss? If you would like I could try and set some time aside and help you with your homework." In this example, you practise empathy, since we never know what's going on in someone's life until after we ask. Even if we have no idea how to help, just knowing that someone is there for us liberates a lot of pressure. This way, you'll be more likely to get an answer on what's troubling them and get to the root of the problem. Like I said earlier, bad grades in the classroom can come in two ways: you can be the best teacher and your class could still be doing horribly; but the opposite is usually the case, since as I mentioned it's not the subject that's fun or boring, it's the teacher. Since the more teachers get feedback from the students, the more they could bring the subject to life, and the more they do that the more students will want to learn. And another pointless thing that school teaches us is that when test day arrives, your teacher would pull apart everyone's desks to "*prevent you from cheating off your friend's answers.*" But this practice just makes students compete with each other because in the end the teacher still expects the same answer.

Teachers need to realize that every student is different, and, naturally, they will have a different thought process for the same question. Most of the time the teacher will only accept a single answer as the correct one, but at the same time, teachers always want the student to produce an original answer. Now I know it's a test and they want to see which students have been paying attention in class, and the only way to do that is by making them take a test individually; that's true. But think of this: what if teachers made everyone work on the same answer together, and made them phrase the answer in their own words; wouldn't that prove that they understand? By doing so, some students will teach their peers things that they didn't understand, in a way that the teacher didn't think of teaching. School tests make you think that there are only a couple of "successful" jobs if you can answer the right question but that's not how life works. Everyone's life and path to success is different, and with that, their way of answering questions will be different too. I know that collective work doesn't always function, but unlike individual test taking and getting marked for your answer, teamwork is an accurate representation of today's world.

Speaking about that, we all know that collaborating with peers is good if you know their intention like how I compare siblings to personal strangers. Since you can't choose them, and their personality will help you choose what type of people you want to attract in your life, it's the same here. The difference is that you both have a common goal which is whatever you are working on, thus just like Luke Hobbs and Deckard Shaw (from the movie *Fast and Furious*) who had to put aside their petty rivalry to save the world, you must learn sometimes that you must set aside how you feel get things done. However, this takes some maturity to do, just watch the movie sequel *Hobbs and Shaw* and you will understand.

Life is the most difficult exam. Many people fail because they try to copy others, Not realizing that everyone has a different question paper.

Teachers also don't take into consideration the future that we are going to live in, as many current jobs will be taken over by machines and artificial intelligence as technology progresses. Schools need to ditch the knowledge-based system and focus more on students' innovation and ability to solve problems, which is increasingly what employers desire out of employees. Besides, we have the internet at our fingertips for any information we need, so we don't need to memorize everything anymore. You can make any student want to learn any topic, or at least keep the interest of a class, if the teachers bring it up in a fun manner.

It's not the theme that's fun or boring, it's all about the teachers' attitude in teaching and how they're committed to the job. Teachers have one of the most important jobs on the planet, because any student can find their passion in the right environment, and they are more likely to develop those interests in the hands of a good teacher. Many teachers will judge a student by the standards that they grew up in and don't realize that what's important to them might not be good for their students. We teach our students from our own experiences, but the lessons we've learned in the past might not be valid in the future since you might study for one thing but then life throws you a curveball and you work someplace else. We need to think ahead and try to learn about the future before teaching it to the students that will be living in it.

Schools also fail at introducing their students to consequences for their behaviour. Of course, actions still have consequences in school, but they are much milder and usually come in the form of either extra work, detention, or a temporary expulsion. The problem with these methods is that they don't effectively change the student's behaviour, and none of these consequences focus on fixing the problems. Another thing, the school also makes students develop an unhealthy relationship with work, where they are told to put up with stress even if the labour is unfulfilling. The four burners theory by David Sedaris explains that we as humans, in our highly demanding society can't have a work/life balance due to the amount of attention we need to give to each class individually since it can't be done together. In the next chapter, you will see how this theory could be applied, each burner represents a class, and the difficulty is trying to stay on top of all of your classes without losing the flow of your school year.

Did you know that dying from a heart attack is most likely to happen on the same day that you get ready to go into a job that you hate? According to an article published by Sunrise Hospital and Medical Center called *"How*

Working Too Much Affects Your Heart"[7], it's due to the excess amount of stress you'll feel. In fact, they state that the effects of overworking are known to be deadly over lengthy periods. A study found that people who work long hours have a twenty-nine percent increased risk of suffering from a stroke. As a study conducted by Harvard found, there was a forty percent increased risk of heart attack or stroke in the first year after retirement.[8] Think of work as building a bed, the more you work and see your progress, the more you'll be tired and want to fall asleep. The way I see it, once you go to sleep, you should be able to sleep peacefully; but the stress of work can even continue into retirement. Instead of sleeping peacefully, you're constantly worrying about finding an extra source of income. And because of inflation, there's a great chance that you will outlive your savings.

We tend to think that once we achieve something, we will find happiness in it, but the reality is that the joy from the achievement is much smaller than it appears. We should instead focus on making ourselves happy with our current living situation and enjoy the path to our achievement which is much longer to go through. The solution to that is either finding a job you love or putting more love into your job because we're likely to spend most of our lives working.

[7,8]*How working too much affects your heart.* Sunrise Hospital and Medical Center. February 17th, 2020,

Even if we make a lot of money, we still aren't necessarily happier if we are still preoccupied with stress and can't find ourselves content with where we are now. Life is like a video game with no "try again" button, since no matter how many levels (years) we're able to survive, once our game is over, we're dead.

Shawn Achor, a Harvard professor found something called the happiness advantage: only ten percent of it comes from the world around us; the other ninety percent comes from how our brains process this world and turn it into a good or terrible experience. He also found that seventy-five percent of job success can be determined by how happy you are, as opposed to smart or talented. When you are happy you can be more optimistic, and stressful events can be dealt with more easily. Furthermore, it was found that creativity, productivity, and intelligence can rise by up to thirty-one percent in happier people, which also makes work easier to deal with.[9] Happiness is an important thing but trying to find what makes you happy is easier said than done. However, it's never too late to try, you just need to be patient with yourself.

The first step to being happy is changing your attitude because a hopeless mind will feed hopeless thoughts. The second step is a change in environment, if you don't like your

[9] YouTube, TEDx Talks, "TEDx Bloomington - Shawn Achor - "The Happiness Advantage: Linking Positive Brains to Performance" June 30th, 2011.

school or workplace, it might be wise to try to move to a new one, as long as you do it with a healthy mindset.

A video by Jay Shetty called *If Work Stresses You Out, Watch This,* shows the unhealthy relationship between a boss and her employee as she abuses her power and fails to do her job. It gets to the point where the employee chooses to quit because he can't stand working for her anymore, leaving her to suffer the consequences. [10] In Jay Shetty's words *"People don't leave their company; they leave their bosses."* According to him, thirty-five percent of people leave because of the stress caused by the bosses and/or managers themselves; seventy-six percent of them leave due to the stress they bring home after a day at work which impacts their relationships; sixty-six percent of people leave due to lack of sleep caused by work-related stress; and sixteen percent leave of stress in general or all three of these factors. He says that stress is contagious, and then, we forget to take care of ourselves. Employers should act more as leaders for their employees instead of just being bosses who order them around. A leader knows how to make everyone feel like part of a team, and when you give the employees more value, they will value their work for the company, and work more efficiently. The second step is taking control of our environment and taking account of our resources to use them to the best of our abilities.

[10,11] YouTube, Jay Shetty, "If work stresses you out, watch this," August 30th, 2019,

When we face a new chapter in our lives, we tend to get stressed, and finding a way to relieve it might require finding tools that work for us. The only person we can truly compare ourselves to is our past selves since that is where we can measure our growth—since you will always find someone in a better situation than you or worse, and we will always be in the middle.

In Japanese culture they say that you have three faces: the first you show the world by masking your flaws; the second you show your friends and family, where you're able to be a bit more vulnerable; and the third you show no one but yourself, exposing all your vulnerabilities and weaknesses. The way you dress can also have a big effect on first impressions; it gives new people an idea of the type of person you are and what you do; I call the first face "professionalism." You have a uniform because you are formed to unify that company, it represents both who you are and whom you identify with, like a school, job, or sports team. The face of professionalism will usually be the first place we look to judge someone, but we should try to hold our expectations because things are not always as they appear. I would like to praise schools that do not impose uniforms on their students. This gives them a greater sense of individuality, promoting more free-thinking instead of "herd mentality" (even though they will still insist that all students can learn the same way). Also, being in an environment that forces you to conform in a way you do not identify with, can bring some stress and confusion.

Bullying

Bullying affects your mental health; it can take a toll on your self-esteem which could lead you to be more socially reserved and can often lead to general unhappiness. Regardless of the severity it still affects you, and since most of the time the school doesn't know about it, there isn't any support to help stop the harassment. Often, you'll have to take matters into your own hands and find a way to stand up to it or suffer in silence. There could be many reasons why someone bullies you but most of the time, it falls into three categories: They want to be you; they see you as a threat to their ego; or they hate themselves.

If they want to be you, chances are they envy you; and to them bullying you will bring you down to their level. In German, "schadenfreude" is a term for finding joy in someone's misfortune. The classic example of this is seen in every high-school movie where bullying is involved; where the nerd who's bullied by a bunch of jocks, usually because the jocks envy the nerd's ability to study and pass his classes. The jocks will rarely admit this, however, because they'd rather create fear in the nerd, and give the illusion that they are the bigger person, even though the nerd has the upper hand overall. Here's where the concept of schadenfreude comes into play because the jock finds pleasure in bullying the nerd, knowing it brings him misfortune. If you've seen the movies *21 and 22 Jump Street*, you'll know that the main characters Schmidt and Jenko became work partners after high school. Because of Schmidt's brains and Jenko's athleticism, they became friends and helped each other get into the police force.

Self-hatred is a concept that causes you to continuously compare your lowest points to everyone else's highlights, and it could affect your self-esteem overall. During those times of comparison, you often feel that the world and everyone around you are living their best lives while you feel like you're wasting your potential. Existential psychologist Rollo May says that,

"The most effective way to ensure the value of the future is to confront the present courageously and constructively." [11] This simple but logical approach seems the best way with dealing with self-hatred, but logic does not always come first to people suffering from mental illness.

The final reason someone could hate you is because they see you as a threat, and that is a defence mechanism on their behalf called "projection." That is when someone projects their insecurities onto you, then claims that you are whatever they're insecure about. Have you ever heard this old saying "sticks and stones may break my bones, but words could never hurt me?" The Mehrabian study, conducted by Albert Mehrabian, shows that words only account for seven percent of communication[12]; so, when it comes to verbal abuse, it's not just the words that are being said, but the way they are

[11] *Inspirational Quotes by Rollo May (American Philosopher).* Inspiration.rightattitudes.com. February 10th 2022,
[13,] Mulder, P. March 7th, 2022. *7 38 55 Rules of Communication.* Toolshero.

interpreted that matters. If a teacher compares your grades in class to another student, you and the teacher hear a different meaning behind what he says.

The teacher is thinking in a way to push you to improve in class, however, what also forms is a competition between you and the student to whom you've been compared. This simply shows how a statement made by the teacher may only have been a passing comment, but it could last in the heart of the student forever.

Now, not only do they have to deal with the fact that they might already have self-esteem issues because of their family dynamic, but now you've added stress. You've added an extra blow to their already beaten back by the pressure at home, in other words, you've added a reason for them to hate school. And all this because you can't come to terms with yourself? You have so much rage inside you that you'd rather take it out on someone who you know can't fight back instead of getting back in the fight with yourself. Because let me remind you that there are only three reasons why you can hate someone and one of them is you. If you already hate yourself, the other two will be tormenting you in the back of your head. You're bullying yourself on what could the other person have that you don't (envy) and because of that, you see them as a threat to your ego or you hate yourselves and project your anger onto them (projection) or you want to be the other person (jealousy).

"It requires greater courage to preserve inner freedom, to move on in one's inward journey into new realms than to

stand defiantly for outer freedom. It is often easier to play the martyr, as it is to be rash in battle[13]."

- Rollo May

The thing that school teaches us is that if someone's bullying you, report it to the principal's office. Believe me, I thought that was the most pointless thing you could teach a child (and I still do), since when you grow up and there's no one there to report to, then what are you going to do? They tell you this to make you learn to respect the law. If someone does something to you and you do nothing back, the blame falls onto them; but if you fight back, you're also in trouble. Now it's obvious that when you're in the playground and someone teases you or calls you names, you can't go around hitting people and then say, "well he started it." The problem comes up however when it is no longer playground teasing and becomes adult manipulation; there isn't anyone to which you can report. Even if you do have an authority figure to talk to, they can do just like the principal did back in school and ignore the harassment from the bully but still tell the victim they can't fight back. Or if you did call the police, they take too long, and you feel as if it's not going anywhere. The problem isn't with the fact that if you get bullied you can't fight back; the problem is that schools don't teach us how to deal with bullying properly.

[13] *Inspirational Quotes by Rollo May (American Philosopher).* Inspiration.rightattitudes.com. February 10th 2022,

Now, on the other hand, teachers or parents might not be aware that their child is a victim of bullying. This can be the case if the child being bullied is either embarrassed about their situation, doesn't have enough trust to talk about it with their parents, or simply want to talk about it would be a burden to others (which it certainly is not). The article *"Children and Bullying"*[14] (free translation) explains it simply: have a conversation. Without hearing the other side of the story, the attempt to bring it up could jeopardize the victim. In this article, they give tips to parents who might struggle to bring up the conversation, regardless of if they have children who are victims of bullying, bullies themselves or witness bullying.

I'm going to share an example. I was eleven years old, playing with a Walmart version of a boomerang, in a park across from the street where I live. When I thew it, two other boys came in and took it from me. After I realized what they did I asked them politely to give it back. Then they started running and as I chased after them, they started laughing since they knew they were faster than me. After a couple of minutes with no success, my mom came from one of the park benches and yelled at the boys to give it back to me, I didn't ask her to intervene she came by herself. She came to help me because she saw that I wasn't achieving what I wanted on my own; I had the right idea I just needed the support

[15] Vie, C. *Les enfants et l'intimidation*. Noovomoi.ca. August 27th 2012,

from the authority of an adult to have the boys stop what they were doing. It might just be my parents. They raised me to try and manage stuff on my own before asking them for help, and to have the right attitude because they wouldn't have helped me more if I would have gone inside crying. This was the only course of action I could have taken because if I had gone inside to get my parents' help, the boys would have already run off and I would have lost my boomerang.

Abuse of Power

Sexual harassment between teachers and students takes place when the teacher abuses their power and takes advantage of their authority. In the same way that anyone at any age can experience some sexual stimulation, whether it's exploration as a child, masturbation or porn as a teenager or a romantic relationship in adulthood; harassment is going to happen somewhere along the line, as there is always a position of authority that can be abused.

During my time in high school, there were a couple of teachers who abused their position of power to take advantage of students. The first one was one of the most beloved teachers around, he was a friendly guy who I even had as a teacher for one of my classes during my last year. He engaged in many school activities, and he especially stood out as the only male teacher in the feminist club at school. I had barely graduated high school when it came out that he was "grooming" girls as young as the age of sixteen as well as sending them unwanted e-mails. When this story broke out it exploded on social media and it shocked many people, and there was even a lot of resistance to accept that he did it because why would he take interest in younger girls if he has a wife and a child. The reason it took the girls who were groomed so long to talk about the story was because they feared they weren't going to be believed, so the fact that there was a lot of resistance sadly validated their fears. If there wasn't so much evidence to support them, it could have even landed them into more trouble, but in this case, the teacher got what he deserved. Unlike the first teacher, however, the second one wasn't very likeable; but he was exceptionally good at his job and had a very strong position of authority over his students. He would always show more favouritism to girls in his class, giving them more compliments on their looks and their grades, he would always touch them on the shoulder when talking to them and just seemed nicer to girls than he was to guys. When I was with Marguerite in that class, she was already warned about how the teacher is a bit creepy and that to not talk to him a lot. However, when she did, he would always give her twice the explanation she needed but compared to when I would talk to him, he would give me half the explanation that I wanted.

To conclude, the schooling environment doesn't teach us **"how to be"** instead they teach us **"what to be,"** and how to act like a "professional." I understand why finding a place in society can be an important thing but asking the question *"what do you want to be when you grow up?"* to a child without them being able to explore what it's like to be a grown-up isn't helpful. As a child, you're just too young to understand what it means to have a job, and the responsibilities that come with it, so it isn't fair to ask that question to children who have no idea what the adult world is like. Yet the answer that you give will still set a standard that might be completely changed as you age and develop. Once you have grown up; you are defined by your job, because it gives an idea of your level of education, as well as your income (that's why the first thing someone asks you as an adult is *"what do you do for a living?"*). What's sad is most of the time we end up in a job we may not like, often because were forced by our parents or the desire to make money. Because of that, many people just don't like their jobs and feel unsatisfied with the work they do. The reality is we aren't guided enough in our youth to know where we'd like to go, and once we reach a point where we could make it's usually too late and often too difficult to change career paths. But now you have this diploma hanging on your wall, stuck in a job with a salary that you depend on, with student debts to pay, and little happiness to show for it. Teachers won't teach us **how** to manage our time, yet they tell us **what** to do with it. They tell us when we get bullied, they tell us not to **fight** back, but won't **defend** us themselves when we ask for their help. They compare their lives to ours and rehearse their favourite line: *"if I could do it, so can you."* Yet they won't show us **how** they did it, they'll just show **what** they did, and expect you to get the same result.

My favourite paradox happens when a teacher is running out of time in class and says:

> *"I don't have to teach you this now, you'll learn it next year anyways."*

But once you reach the next year, your teacher is already expecting you to know that exact thing you were never taught. They always return to you with:

> *"I shouldn't have to explain this; you learned it last year."*

Well, guess what? There is not a race to learn something, to make sure you properly understand something so you can build from a solid foundation. Teachers should not be rushed to fill in a curriculum but be focused on making sure the children properly know the content of the current year so that they won't be suffering through the next. A little revision never hurts and as they always say, *"two steps forwards and one step back."* Not only do they fail to manage their own time, but they also fail at teaching it to us as well. Every year they love to tell us that it's going to get harder and harder, but they fail to show us how to maintain ourselves during those times (and not being able to manage their own time shows us that they are failing at it as well). That, and if you think about it no one teaches you time management, they just expect you to know what to do and how to prioritize your work without any help.

When you're on the job, let's suppose that it's something that you studied for, got a certain degree, and now you're working in that field. They won't assume that you know how to use all the machinery, theory, terminology, etc. even if you studied in that domain, because every institute requires different skills. Even when you get a promotion, you still need to go over the responsibilities of your new position, since they've changed from your last one. On the biggest scale, if you've immigrated to another country, acquiring a job is an even greater challenge because of varying standards in education. The main issue I see with high school is that as you go through it, they're supposed to give you an idea of what you want to be; but how are you supposed to find what's right for you when school enforces a rigid schedule you barely have a say in?

While students should be given guidance through high school it shouldn't restrain them from exploring new environments and studying new things they might like. Schools should be more proactive at modelling education around the child, and not the other way around because otherwise we lose what interests us, and we end up conforming to the system to work through it, but we also lose a part of ourselves in the process. Chances are, if your parents have immigrated here, they forced a path onto you; and it's the path they think they would have chosen if they were born in Canada. In other words, they mould you into someone that they couldn't be once upon a time and project their dreams onto their children to live them through them.

If school is really preparing us for **our** future, allow **us** to choose the classes that we identify with and care more about. Then the selection of high school courses should function like in college or university, as in you choose a program you want, with classes related to that program and your preferred time to have them.

If there's a subject that you know you want to learn about, you shouldn't have to wait until high school to finally learn about it while having to deal with a bunch of other classes you don't care about in the meantime. What you should be able to do is pick a domain, and within it have courses related to what you picked to allow for more exploration of a specific subject without the commitment of college or university education. This allows students to explore new domains, especially things they might not be good in without it compromising their future (like MATH: Mistakes Allows Thinking to Happen). I know there's the whole idea of *"we're just making sure that children don't close any doors of opportunity"* but I say no to that philosophy because children who already have an idea shouldn't have their dreams squashed by a "safety net". Would you rather walk through the door you're not invited to or knock on the closed door of the place you know you belong? Well, I don't think the second door should be closed at all; I think it's unfair that a student has to break through a closed door just so that they can make the right decision.

Regardless of what you do with your time and money, there's always a choice you have to make and sometimes you think twice about the other choice and over-analyze if that was the better one. That being said, *"You don't pay to go to work since you get paid, unlike school you pay to go, and you've not secured a job afterwards."*

What that means is you need to make sure you are capitalizing on your education (pun intended), to make sure you have your money's worth. Just like anything else you buy, you want to make sure it's worth it; but with school, you're also spending something more valuable than money which is time. So, when you see that either you're not getting your money's worth, or you have other things in mind; you might get bored, change programs, drop out, or don't invest yourself fully in what's being taught to you.

When it comes to dropping out, your parents or teachers won't see it as a great idea, since to them it's important to have a good education. However, the people who see dropping out as a sad thing, well they have to realize that whoever decides to drop out did so because the school system already didn't work for them. Because like a job, if you get fired or decide to leave but you have a responsibility towards a family then you need to make sure that you have a plan B. Like my dad likes to say: *"If you don't have a plan, you are planned to fail."* Because the money you spend on your education will be gone a long time before you can make it back; and the time you spend getting that money, is something you will never get back. To quote the famous

Albert Einstein, *"Education is what remains after one has forgotten what one has learned in school[15]."*

Do you know where you are most likely to experience burnout? In school, jobs, and relationships. This is because it's in these places that you will invest yourself to the fullest, trying to satisfy someone else and then you forget to take care of yourself. Schools and jobs have neglected mental health, for instance, jobs do everything they can to make the workplace physically safe, to avoid lawsuits and schools, regularly practise lockdowns and fire drills for emergencies. But truly little focus is placed on mental health, resulting in mental illness being unnecessarily difficult to deal with in the workplace. Your mental health and physical health are equally important, even if you can spot one easier than the other, this doesn't mean it affects you less, and that one is more important than the other. Instead, mental health shouldn't be something to make into a special occasion, but something to be constantly worked on. I understand that in some cultures, the idea of mental health is even seen as taboo; and the problem with this is that many teachers and employers who are brought up in these cultures don't see the importance of learning about it and informing themselves. However, the only reason something is "taboo" is because you were never taught about it, or you don't know how to

[15] "Albert Einstein Quotes About School | A-Z Quotes". *A-Z Quotes*, 2021,

bring it up. So, just saying that something is taboo, is because you were never educated on the importance of it.

During my winter semester at college for social work, I had a class called "group therapy." For our last evaluation, we were split into seven teams and each team had to produce a metaphor to explain the consequences of a subject that we were assigned. Therefore, two of my classmates were given low self-esteem and they brought in two identical apples. The first student showed us the first apple and told us to complement it then asked how we felt. Afterwards, the other student came with another apple and told us to insult the apple then she also asked us how we felt. Then they proceeded to cut the apple that we complimented, and it was ripe, but when they cut the apple that we insulted, it was rotten. We forget that by consuming the negative thought of other people, on the outside we look good, but we feel bad on the inside.

Problem 2

No Room for Autonomy

School gives us so much work, but not the time management skills to deal with it. From not being able to learn what you want, to the bells that control when you go in or out of class or in and out of school. Whatever it is the schooling system doesn't give us enough freedom. You have pre-made schedules, filled with the amount of classes required for your academic year, even when it comes to those "elective classes" you still need to take them since you need a certain number of classes for that year. Even if you get to choose which class you elect (pun intended) and don't like it, you could remove it but the class that you would like has to be offered within the time slot of the class you don't want, or you risk messing up your schedule. However, in college, your classes are all over the place and you have no control over the class you're going to have, nor the time it's offered. If somehow your schedule changes, they don't notify you and you need to deal with it.

Therefore, elective classes are "mandatory optional" meaning you have the choice of which class to take but you are forced to choose one of them to fill the remaining holes in your schedule. In the last Problem, if you want a child to like going to school and make them love learning, give them something they want to learn. Even if it's not offered in their year, I can tell you that I suffered through a lot of classes before I actually liked school as a whole. In college it's the same thing, you have a program with specific classes and on top of that you need to take an elective class per trimester because it's mandatory optional. However, when it comes to class selection in university, even if you're promised so many opportunities, to benefit from the so-called "student life" because your course loads are too heavy you can't capitalize off them.

Picture this, you want to be a psychologist; regardless of the reason, since it shouldn't matter as long as you know why, and don't lose sight of that. You're in eighth grade, and you can't take anything related to psychology until you're in high school. In the meantime, you need to go through all this math, sciences, history, and every other class that isn't of any interest to you.

On top of that, you have the pressure of your teachers, and your parents expecting good grades from you. The problem is, you're not applying yourself because none of the classes interest you and you're not going to want to continue. But they don't know that you have other things in mind because even the path put in place is made to keep doors open for students, not every student can go down the same path and find the same opportunity at the end of the road. Even if your school does offer a class in your field of interest, it might be offered too far down the "path" that's already been carved for you by the school. The later years of high school usually offer more classes to choose from, but the problem is, by this point the time is running out to choose what you want to do after you graduate. You tell kids to chase their dreams, but how can they do that when schools ban them from finding that dream to start with?

And a consequence of a pre-made schedule, or too many extra-curricular activities is that you have very little time for yourself. The way I see "me-time" would be any time that you're not in class or doing something for a class either during the week or weekend, therefore during school recess is the only time you get to yourself. Since even if you do summer school and get credited for all the classes, your summer is taken up by things that you could have been doing during the school year. On the other hand, they don't allow you to either take independent measures to get your homework done. Teachers should allow students to have study periods in class once they are given their homework. This would allow us to work on the material we've just learned while it's still fresh and give us less to do once we come home from school. Teachers wouldn't let me, but then when they are available for us, and we don't make use of it they blame us for being irresponsible.

For those teachers who think they're teaching time management by punishing us when our homework is turned in late, they're wrong since it won't stop the behaviour from happening because it's a negative reinforcement tool. But when it's them, they're allowed to say, *"I have three classes of twenty students and sixty tests to correct"* and we have no choice but to excuse them. Come on teacher you chose this class and the work. If you can't live up to it, don't make us do it either. Meaning, instead of giving an amount of work based on our capacity, give an amount that's reasonable knowing that you'll have at least two to three times more to correct. So, you want us to live up to your policy of over-due homework or project by not wanting to correct it if it's late by a certain number of days, but then it's hypocritical to expect us to forgive you when our grades are late by two to three weeks. In the same way, you have more than one class to teach, with homework, tests, and projects to give, and correct. We have more than one to attend with homework, tests to complete and homework to turn in.

Now this is sad, and I think it's something that needs to be addressed since I didn't learn the proper use of an agenda until I was in the seventh grade, but teachers love giving homework as early as fourth grade. But agendas are one of the most effective ways to manage your time. It's visual, you could plan your days, weeks, or month, and if it's electronic you could set it up so it could remind you of a specific event at a specific time. I know some people will say *"better late than never;"* however, I say it should be taught earlier since you get an agenda as soon as you start school. Teachers, I'm talking to you here. Teach us how to manage our time, by using our agendas and you would hear fewer excuses for over-due assignments or homework. As far as I can remember, the only teacher that taught me how to manage my time at school is my seventh-grade elementary teacher. She taught us how to use our agendas appropriately; she would make us write down our homework and events and how long it would take to complete them in our agendas after school for the week. For example, my schedule back in the day would be something like this: Monday, nothing; Tuesday, jujitsu from 7:30 to 8 pm; Wednesday, piano from 5 to 5:30 pm; Thursday, jujitsu from 7:30 to 8 pm; and Friday, nothing. From there she'd be able to help us deal with the amount of homework she'd give us according to our schedule. If we take mine for example, I know that I would have more time on Mondays and Fridays than any other day. But everyone's schedule is different, so what she would do is come see each of us and say:

"Okay now with the homework you have tonight, show me where you plan to spend most of your time… now write it down."

She did that so then we could visually see on paper what we had to do and how much time we had to do it and she was able to see where we had time. If ever we'd say something, she knew that we knew that we couldn't lie since what we had to do for that night was already written down. I understand that not everyone will guide you every step of the way as she did, but for me, having my teacher actively participate in teaching me how to manage my time made me more confident in organizing myself in the future since I have the tools to do it.

According to psychologists Dan Pink and Peter Gray *"Autonomy is an innate psychological need, but children don't like school because they are not free"*[16]. And because of that, the education system is sending a dangerous message to children—that they are not in control of their own lives. Children in the earlier years of school of course need to be guided in the right direction, but taking complete control of their decisions could harm their autonomy as they grow up and they feel as comfortable taking care of themselves. However, the problem is that when you advance in your schooling, you're forced to understand how things work, and you become more self-sufficient. Meaning that once you leave school you need to know how to manage your own time, which is something you can't learn when all your time is managed for you. Now I know what some adults are thinking, *"welcome to the real world,"* I hate that because it shows that adults don't think that school struggles are a real-world problem. And sure, if it's telling children that when they have a job, they have a supervisor that tells them what to do and when, and manage their time for them, then I

---

[16] YouTube, Next school, "6 problems with our school system", December 15th, 2016

understand what the school system is trying to do. However, for one unlike at your work, once children get home, they have someone else to take orders from, and that is their parents. Also, since the world is rapidly changing, when it comes to time management, we have tools, so we don't need someone breathing down our necks, because that means we're always going to rely on you for everything and don't tell me that's what you want.

What I don't understand about the school system is that it was made for you to think critically, except about what you learn. You can't ask why you learn something, or how it will impact your future, but *somehow it will*. School is supposed to be designed to promote creativity, I don't know about you but after four years of high school I felt as if I'd learned the same basic things over and over again. It's similar to saying students are encouraged to pursue their dreams…As long it's within what they offer because if not, it's not "worth it" or deemed "meaningful" according to them. Or when teachers encourage you to think outside the box…however it must fit inside their slightly smaller box or else they begin to judge you, for being misguided. The school system functions like the prison system in this respect, boxing you into its strict timetable and making you do what it tells you to. They make you use your brain, but only in the way they want you to use it; and the little freedoms they do give you are still locked into the choices they offer you.

School System Vs. Juvenile System

Your children have not committed any crimes, yet the school system thinks the opposite. The methods of discipline, and conformity that schools enforce on children, are not as far from the world experience by criminal adults. Let us get down to business.

At my elementary school, there were fences everywhere, with people who were hired to supervise us kids during lunch and when our teachers weren't there. We barely got to do what we wanted apart from when we had recess. When I was in eighth grade, the whole school was playing soccer, but it would always be annoying if the ball would go over the fence, we would either have to wait until someone passes by and gets it or ask a teacher to go get it and they may, but if they didn't, we weren't allowed to go and get it, even if it's the end of recess teachers still wouldn't allow us to go and get it. Now I know that laws stop the school from allowing kids to get off the property, but these laws also stop kids from being independent, even for really simple things. If you think of it, that's sad because the school doesn't take into consideration that we're in eighth grade and we've already learnt that we have to look both ways before crossing the street.

My elementary school was based upon the Steiner-Waldorf approach to learning, for those who aren't well to simply put it, you learn things through arts, stories, nature, songs, and anything creative. The approach itself was discovered by Rudolf Steiner and it was based upon a few

42

things such as artistic activities and imagination, reason for all the arts singing eurythmy and stories. First and foremost, it is supporting a student-centred approach to learning and tries to offer a safe for students to explore its learning environment. It is also supposed to make us develop students to be socially acceptable and economically responsible, the reason for students' integration in the winter and spring fairs or making soup for the rest of the school if we wanted to raise funds for school outings. Another thing that is worth mentioning is the Steiner-Waldorf approach aims to create a routine and stability in what is being taught. So, what would happen is that there was this one teacher that was the head of all teachers, and he designed the curriculum for each class since he has taught them all over the years with his class. Also, to reinforce stability if the teacher wants and the schoolboard approves of the teacher's work, they could keep teaching their class the main subjects such as Science, Language, Art, Geography, and History for the next grades. This way creates a bond between the teacher and the students and even if the teacher does not have all the abilities, they could at least do their best to transmit what they know to their students in a way that promotes understanding.

Consequently, any new teacher or teachers that do not know what or how to teach could go to him and he'll help since it's all the same to help them teach and move forwards with their class. The Steiner-Waldorf approach is centred upon three child development periods: The early years where the focus is learning through play, and developing your five senses, the lower school is when you get the core school subject like Science, Language, Art, Geography, and History while leaving out the sports until next year. The focus is understanding the subject, so the idea is to take one and focus on it for at least a month and don't focus a lot on grades. Most schools don't go up to eighth grade but mine did and that's when you get the last developmental stage and that's the upper school. At this point, if you're still in a school that has the Steiner-Waldorf approach, this last stage is focused on bringing the child to think independently and you have specialized teachers for each subject like high school. [17]

I first came to the school at the age of six and my first-grade teacher was amazing. She really left an impact on me, so even if she was my teacher up until third grade, I knew that I had a good start to school with an amazing teacher. We did a lot of arts, such as watercolour, knitting, and drawing. When it came to learning things such as the alphabet or how to play the recorder it was always introduced with a song, or a story and those stories would always involve fictional characters. There was this activity called the lantern walk, it was done outside at night and the story was that St Nick lost his donkey and we needed to find him by calling his name or singing a song. Or when it came to explaining to us why it snows during winter, there was this whole story about how mother nature and the winter king would battle for the earth.

[17] Symes, J. *Waldorf Steiner - Progressive Education*. Progressive Education, February 5th February 2020,

So, when it was winter, he would blow all over the ground with his icy breath and just like that, winter was there. And when spring finally sprung it was all mother nature and her earthly children who would help her to get rid of the winter and that would just happen back and forth. However, these were fables, and it was through those fables that we would learn lessons such as sharing, helping, and caring for one another; or the famous *Tortoise and the Hare* with "slow and steady wins the race" demonstrating reliance and perseverance.

Given the fact that the teachers were not specialized in a particular subject and the learning is more generic, the parents were able to help their children and actively participate in their academic journey. What I really appreciated from that approach was the community we build inside the school, meaning that the parents who came in to help regularly, had an important impact on every child. For example, there were a couple of parents including my mother who used to go and help out at the school and from that they were able to know what was going on academically with their child and provide help if necessary. Whenever it was someone's birthday, we would do a little potluck among our class, as well as siblings or friends from other classes, including the parents and that was the only time that we'd be able to share our lunch since normally we're not allowed and more often than not, we'd be served snacks. The only time I was able to play something I wanted was when I was in third grade, I would see the older kids playing soccer and I wanted to play with them. They would always let me, but if I got caught by one of my classmates and they would tell my teacher they would stop me from playing because I was too young to play the sport and being with the older kids did not make it better.

A teacher that really changed my way of learning in school was my teacher from fourth to sixth grade. He gave us some basic house rules of the classroom, and chores with a "best child of the month" system, for positive reinforcement. He would write out every student's name on the chalkboard, and any time we did something good, either individually or collectively, we'd gain a certain amount of checkmarks. At the end of each month, he would go to Dollarama and buy things out of pocket for everyone and give them to the person who had the most checks. He also read us stories from his home country and showed us funny videos about what we were learning. The best of all was that he introduced us to the world of sports, and from grades four to six we participated in soccer tournaments. At the time when we were playing sports, we'd often match up boys versus girls, it was fair since even if most of the boys were faster, stronger, and more skilled, there were twice as many girls in the class, and we were competitive so doing boys versus girls just made everything a lot simpler and fun. He gave us a positive window to look at, through sports, African stories, fun chores, and surprises at the end of the month. There was even one time in fourth grade when we went to Calypso water park to eat out at a buffet in Québec. What I find funny is that the teacher I'm talking about felt bad about not being able to give us the Waldorf approach because for one he didn't come from Canada, he came from Ivory Coast, and second of all he didn't know what the whole approach was about, but he was willing to learn. Therefore, what he would do when we had art classes the oldest teacher would teach us. We also formed a choir with the higher grades of our school led by the teacher of the oldest grade, and we would sing every day after recess for ten minutes altogether, from grades four to eight.

When I got to high school, my experience was different, and the learning approach was very generic. To start, teachers have fewer chances to create a bond with the students because they don't follow them to their next class since the teacher is specialized in one subject. Also, at times a teacher has to teach multiple classes at multiple levels and that could diminish the quality of learning for the students since they have so many children to teach so they can't appeal to everyone's particular needs. Meaning that the parents have to step in and that can't always happen, especially if your needs aren't in the majority. But, unlike my elementary school, there's a sort of separation between the parent and the student so whenever the parent tries to intervene it's unmotivating and it's the last they want to do since the school tries to limit the parent involvement as much as possible so when things aren't done right, there's a lack of trust and respect coming from the parents, criticizing the school system. As opposed to middle school, where the different teachers come to you in your homeroom, and you have everything on your desk, so it makes it so much easier. In high school, you need to find your next class and you often have to run, because you have ten minutes until the next bell to get to your locker, get what you need, and go to your next class. When it comes to lunchtime you have an hour and you have fewer restrictions on what you could eat because yes there's a cafeteria and there's a variety of things to choose from when it comes to lunchtime, but it might not be healthy or if it is it's more expensive.

Another thing about high school is that I didn't have a lot of school outings, either because I didn't sign up for a lot of clubs or because my school was just underfunded. However, we did host a lot of sporting events, and since I was part of the soccer team, I played against a lot of different schools. People say that a student shouldn't sign up for too many extra circular activities because it could affect their schoolwork and well-being. Because it allows students to explore their interests without the pressure of grades or the school system behind it. For example, the way that I was able to go to France and England in eighth grade because my class was responsible for funding our trip. Also, if we talk about the school presidency, students are able to understand the basics of democracy and the responsibility of having a campaign by understanding each role and how to influence people to get their votes. However, we have to remember that in most public schools, there isn't too much funding so most extracurricular activities and the teachers or parents who animate them are doing volunteer work, meaning that they aren't getting much support financially.

On to another concern, teachers, listen up. I also don't understand the concept of escorting us to the bathroom during exams, I mean what kind of cheating do you think is going on in a school bathroom. Trust us, if we need to go, we will go since the information we have can't sink in when we have to use the bathroom (pun intended).

First of all, you make us leave our phones in class, and it's not like we're hiding our manuals in the bathroom stalls. And, If I ask to go to the washroom during an exam or test, you can't just assume while I'm going to the washroom, I took a detour to my locker and looked at my notes, therefore there's no need to escort us. Second of all, if we really wanted to cheat that way, escorting us to the bathroom isn't going to help much in resolving that issue. Since we know that each test and exam will impact our final grade and we're older, so we know what the consequences of cheating are. You teachers have the bigger end of the stick, even if the bigger end of penalties falls on us, if we'd cheat on a test or you suspect plagiarism then all you have to do is give an F with a valid reason.

Third, since we can't use our phones during tests, how do you expect us to even talk to anyone? In jail cells, the bathroom is inside the cell so if we got to go then we just do it. Since you can't tell us to go to the bathroom, our bladders do that already, and it's our right to relieve ourselves if we need to. And I know that for safety reasons you want to make sure that there aren't too many people outside of class at the same time. Often leaving class is also seen as distracting and embarrassing for the student, because permission is needed anytime someone leaves class. I suggest setting up a system for leaving class instead, where a student signifies to the teacher that they are going without having to announce it to the world. Writing your name on the board, or simply using a hand signal to show the teacher you're leaving class, are methods that teachers already use today in some classrooms, but really, they should be the standard for everyone. The same applies to the teacher as well, you shouldn't need to wait until we're doing a test or independent work to use the washroom, if you got to go then go.

I know that the more "important" the class is, the less you want us to leave. In other words, if it's a period where you're teaching a lesson to the class, you'll want us to stay in class and listen more than during study periods where we work on our own. Students shouldn't fear missing something crucial just because they miss class for five minutes. During study periods, the teacher should go over the things that were missed with students who didn't understand, or those who were absent on bathroom breaks. In a large classroom, it's natural that not everyone understands the first time, so the teacher should expect to go over something more than once to get everyone on the same page.

When you first ask a child what they want to be when they grow up, they'll normally say something that looks cool; simply because they have a vivid imagination or it's something they might look up to. As the child ages and matures, however, its passions and interests will also mature. Their abilities, options, and interests will be more important for deciding their future career path rather than just what sounds cool. Because if one person says that they want to be a doctor but hates the idea of going to medical school, I'm sure we can agree the more they study in the field the more they might hate it, and the less they'd want to become a doctor. Since having to study medicine, the less they will want to become a doctor and the worse of a doctor they will become. On top of that, think about it, if you become something that you don't want to be, not only are you doing yourself a favour by not torturing yourself into all these extra studies that you never wanted to do in the first place. But you did because you've been told over and over and over again that doing so will give you a "successful life." You're doing a favour for the world because you're eliminating one less potential unskilled doctor in the workspace, and it will prevent deadly accidents.

In the last Problem, I talked about why we should ask "who you want to be" and not "what you want to be." The reason is because, if your qualities and passion are not in line with the future job you want you might not be satisfied with yourself. I was thinking, what if influencing us into wanting a job that pays well is something that's implicitly taught by the schooling system? Jobs that are associated with art, sports, or anything else where the pay rate is unstable, will be judged by the school system for being an "irresponsible" idea because getting a significant amount of money to make a living will take time and patience to build. Jobs that require creativity can't just be forced, as that creativity has to come naturally; sports demand a lot of practice, and hours of dedication before seeing any results as opposed to contractual jobs which usually offer the much safer route of payroll and a linear amount of productivity each week. Therefore, when they say a job is "stable," what they mean is you'll be paid for your work or when they say it's "unstable," it's because the amount you get paid is based on your performance which could vary from person to person and from day to day.

If the school system is pushing for students to get into worldwide known colleges, and then pushing them to get into high-paying jobs, to be able to have financial freedom but after a certain time, you'll have to repay the loan you took for your fees and you better be interested to pay it or else they add those financial interests (pun intended). It's one thing to push a student to want to get into a high-paying job since you know that they'll be well off financially and in this modern world, you can't get anywhere with no money. But it's completely another thing if you push a student to want to go into a worldly recognized college or university to then have a high-paying job because you think that whatever they want to b is not going to "pay the bills" or "pay the school fees." And it's also wrong to remove a student's creativity and freedom just to assure their safety as a "dog in society". In case you haven't noticed, I didn't specify which high-paying job a teacher would want a student to pursue, because if teachers want students to be well-off financially then they should know that athletes get paid very well and a medical neurosurgeon gets paid very well and have two different lifestyles; so, it comes down to what the student's abilities and how they use that to benefit themselves. But if it's for the other reason, you'll push a student to want to be a medical neurosurgeon since there's a clear glorified path.

Teachers claim they prepare their students for the future, yet if the school system itself barely changes, how are the teachers supposed to proceed? The world is constantly changing, and yet the school system remains constant, just like a prisoner who is stuck in the past, watching the present and future pass them by. In the world that we live in, we need people that can do the opposite of what factory workers are conditioned to. Look back at the Finnish school system and see how advanced they are; they keep their schools up to date and it allows their people to be looking ahead.

One of the biggest ways that schools still use industrial-age methods for learning is seen in the grading system. Grades are not used as a measure of understanding for students, that's just how it is described on paper. The grading system of standardized tests only provides a very rough estimation for comprehension because it emphasizes specific questions. This means people who understand the concepts can still fail in isolated instances, and these tests do not take into account people's different mindscts when tackling questions. These tests focus on a single way of thinking (usually the teacher's) and punish those who think differently with lower grades and with that, fewer opportunities.

The problem doesn't stop at school though, since parents were taught in the same system, and see school the same way. They push their child to do well in classes even when the school system does the bare minimum to help them along the way. It's like the expression *"You can bring a horse to the water, but you can't force him to drink,"* it's the same thing, you can bring a child to school but you can't force him to learn. Well, if you put some sugar in the water then the horse will like it more. The same idea can work for students, they just have to be shown how learning is a good thing and can be made enjoyable, where learning becomes a natural by-product rather than the focus. The focus on failure should not be present in learning, because that's what stops students from participating in the first place. They should not be ridiculed for a bad answer and should be pushed to find the right one on their own. The hill to success shouldn't be made steeper for those who already struggle to climb it.

Teachers should be paid fairly for the work they do, considering the critical role they play in society. Their work will influence the future of countless children, and they should be fairly compensated for it. Good teachers are often being made to sacrifice their pay for their students instead of being given better support as many teachers often buy supplies from their own pockets to fund a higher quality of education for their students. This causes a system that limits a teacher's ability to improve the quality of education, rather than supporting it. This is the big reason it's illegal to make private schools in Finland, as rich parents can fund the schools and it benefits everyone.

When I was in elementary school, we had two teachers for multiple subjects. When my eighth-grade teacher would change subjects from Math to English, she would erase whatever she would have written on the board in the previous lesson without even checking if we had written it down or not. If we complained she would say *"Stop complaining because in high school they don't give you time to write things down, and it will be twice the length of this."*

The problem is that once I got to high school, I realized I had **twice as much** homework in eighth grade than I would throughout my **whole** high school years combined. My teacher wanted to expose me to more homework to prepare me, but more importantly, she also taught us the time management skills necessary to complete the work on time, which was the actual lesson we learned. But unlike in high school, like when my eleventh-grade English teacher told us to write a five-paragraph essay by the end of the period, and we all complained about how it was too much to write in such a short amount of time. She would just giggle and respond, *"Oh so you think this is hard, well wait until you get to college, and they ask you for five full pages!"* and then you'll learn about my college experience in the conclusion.

For example, how the COVID-19 pandemic switch everything and I got to learn things I wanted but not in the appropriate circumstances, which made my motivation for college drop progressively.

Now there's no problem preparing children for the next step in their education, the problem is that they give us an image of the future when they keep telling us it'll get harder and harder, but it also implies that we shouldn't be struggling with whatever we are currently going through. They are minimizing our problems in the present trying to prepare for the ones in the future, which in itself can do more harm than good. In the end, don't minimize someone's hardships just because you were able to overcome them. The reason becoming a teacher is so hard in Finland is because of the test you have to take in order to be a teacher. To be a teacher in Finland you need to pass an entrance examination which consists of three parts. The first part of the exam was reading, comprehension and memorizing. The second part has to do with preparing a small activity for the university students to take part in as if you were a teacher. The examinators are looking for communication amongst everyone involved, teamwork, and how creative the examinees in planning how they are going to give their class. Finally, the third part is a formal interview with a couple of supervisors from the master's degree program, who ask the students studying to become teachers some questions. *"In the master's degree program, you have 5-6 years of studying on anything in a teacher education program but in Finland, they also study curriculum planning, assessment, and evaluations as part of the work. As well as school improvement, special education, leadership, and many other things are included in this master's degree program* "[18].

You can imagine why teachers are given so much freedom in Finland because they know what they are doing, and the parents can trust the teachers in teaching their kids what they need in a manner that they could understand. In Finland, the teachers are in charge of making their curriculum. Think of it, since the teachers get to create their learning environment, which means more Individual Learning Plans (IEP), and that means more students are going to succeed since the teachers know first-hand what their students need. Teachers can also go the extra mile because of good funding, and since they are fully in control of how the curriculum is delivered, personally, I think that's a recipe for success. It's similar to a registered social worker (RSW), they see your suffering by you simply wanting their services, they understand your difficulties because you've explained it to them, and they've asked a significant amount of questions to better their understanding. Now they're in full control to go over an intervention plan with you so you can reach your goal as they are fully independent in their methods of problem-solving.

[19,] YouTube, WISE, "What if Finland's Great Teachers Taught in Your Schools?" August 8th, 2014,

In prison, when you walk in, you are told to take off your clothes and put on a uniform; you are given a number which defines your identity; and the only way to succeed is to blindly follow orders until you are released into the world. The crazy thing is, can you tell the differences between a school and a prison, or are they starting to look the same? School strips you of your originality and makes you conform. The significant difference is how people outside perceive you: In prison, you are looked at with anger and disappointment for having ruined your life; while in school people see a happy child with every opportunity in front of them (even if many of those opportunities have already been taken away by the school itself)

- *"Prisoner 24601 come forwards."*

- *"I have a name."*

- *"In here, that number is your name."*

Does that remind you of anything else than the opening scene from *Les Misérables*? In the musical, Javert treats Jean-Valjean by disregarding the fact that he has a name, by emphasizing the importance of the number on his suit like he's some sort of property. There's also the fact that Jean-Valjean reminds Javert that he has a name, but Javert doesn't correct himself and instead tells Valjean he has a name as well and to never forget it. This system expects the student to know the authority figure's name and associate it with their identity; the authority then does the opposite with the students, by removing their identity and leaving them only with a number. This minimizes the importance of the student in the situation and puts the focus more on their results on paper.

Speaking of stripping away originality, the public school system responds by removing cookie-cutter uniforms to diversify people's identities. However, these systems still represent restrictive measures in the form of dress codes that the schools use to prejudice certain stereotypes. For example, you weren't allowed to wear any piece of clothing, or jewellery that had any suspicion of racism, sexism etc. You also can't wear headbands since they would associate it with being with a gang or pretending to be part of being Muslim. The dress code was invented to restrict the clothes you wear, as they can reveal some things about you, like your background and attitude. When it comes to a workplace, we want the customers to see some sort of unity within the institution that demonstrates that each employee shares the mission of the place, and it just looks clean. However, by imposing a sort of dress code in public schools they favour some stereotypes over others, but their reasoning might not be very reasonable. I'm sure that a lot of girls feel that the dress code in public schools restricts girls from wearing things they would be comfortable with into wearing more conservative clothing not because it's not appropriate, it's from the misogynistic idea that it'll just be too "provocative" for guys.

For example, women weren't allowed to wear tank tops if the straps were thinner than three fingers, shorts that were shorter than the mid-thigh and leggings were allowed to be worn as a very controversial topic. Also, on a collective database, The Pudding done on 481 schools, thirty-two to ninety-seven items have been banned and it so happens to be the same clothing you would wear in summer. [19] PBS NewsHour Student Reporting Labs discussed with the children from Etiwanda High School to get their opinions on their school's dress code Some students feel that boys can get away with more things than girls, and others feel that if a student breaks the code and is sent home, it doesn't do anything to support their education.

[19] Thomson, A., Thomson, K., & Houston, A. The Pudding. February 2019. "The Sexualized Messages Dress Codes are Sending to Students"

A YouTube video made by Vox called: _Teaching in the US vs. the rest of the world_[20], compares two people who graduated college and now want to teach in middle school. According to them, Anna the recent graduate from America will have a harder time than Sofia the Finland graduate and because of that Anna's chances of leaving are twice as higher than Sofia's. Demands not high for teachers, what is the result of fewer teachers and more students, does this mean there are no rising student rates in Finland, etc.

One of the main reasons why teachers in the United States quit their job is the number of hours they have to work a day, a total of forty-six hours a week—that's an hour and a half more work a day than the average workday of teachers in the Organization of Economic Development (OECD) which is an organization that tries to build better policies and promote equal work opportunity. In South Korea, Finland and Israel, teachers work thirty-three hours a week, meaning that teachers in the US have to work up to two and a half hours more every day. Teachers in Japan however work a total of fifty-six hours a week, that's more than two hours a day than the teachers in the US. The problem is the number of hours spent preparing activities, grading, and creating tests is far greater than the time that the teachers spend teaching the students. That gives a teacher a certain amount of time to teach and whether the students understand or not,

---

[20] YouTube, Vox, "Teaching in the US vs. the rest of the world", January 11th, 2020,

isn't their top priority. Instead, if teachers would spend less time creating tests or exams that focus on their way of thinking and more time teaching those students who are often behind because of their grades, those teachers would see an improvement because the time is spent on what matters and that's the student.

Teachers in those countries get more time to collaborate, grade the tests, and plan the way to teach the class. An advantage is that students in the US scored a higher average in the PISA examination in 2018 which consists of reading, science, and math than the OECD average, but still scored lower than the students in Finland, Singapore, Japan, and South Korea, where teaching hours are much lower. According to Vox, Anna would spend more time in a classroom teaching, planning, grading, and attending after-school activities but wouldn't get paid more than Sofia who spends an hour and a half less. The last element that would make Anna leave is the view on teachers in America vs Finland in their respective countries. Now I don't need to say why the teachers in Finland are highly respected in the country because I talked about it earlier, but since the US doesn't spend a lot of money on education funds, people in America also don't respect their teachers and the education system as a whole.

Now for the cherry on the Sundae, my friend Pierce took a criminology class in university and showed me a video called: *To Kill or to Cure*[21] comparing prison systems in four countries: China, Japan, the United States, and Finland. In China, it's simple: just like their schools are hard on discipline, it's the same with their prisons. China is the world's leading country for capital punishment, where you could be executed for murder, bank robbery, and political corruption among other laws that are considered equally severe in the Chinese justice system. China was not always a system that had such brutal enforcement of the death penalty, however as the country grew rapidly throughout the twentieth century, so did the crime rates, which eventually caused reform in the judicial system. The government implemented the "strike hard" system; tackling the criminals head-on with extreme methods of punishment in an attempt to scare the criminals. This system has been implemented since 1983 and has been widely criticized for its ineffective results in lowering criminal behaviour. However, the system's continued use of this system to this day is partly the reason China is the leading country in the number of executions per capita worldwide. *"Many Chinese leaders fear that they are sitting on top of a powder cake and that social order is not a natural thing in Chinese society. If they don't take strong measures to fight crime on a regular basis, the social order could easily degenerate into chaos,"* [22] says

[22, 23, 24, 25, 26,] Freed, Josh, and Jon. Kalina. To Kill or to Cure : Parts 1 & 2. Galafilm Productions, 2002.

Murry Scott Tanner, a Professor at Western Michigan University.

The way that they instill fear in the population is that the criminal is paraded in the streets before being put down; and they often display hundreds of executions at once, through the method of a bullet through the head. The system is also designed to make trials as quick as possible, which often leads to many unjust trials to complete them quickly. This prison system is it's based on fear, it commands respect and order while trying to restore justice, a reflection of their rigid schooling system. Man, woman, or child, you get the same result, you commit a crime…you're dead, you get convicted for a crime, regardless of if you're innocent or guilty…you're dead.

Moving towards the West, the criminal justice system in the United States is not any less flawed than it is in China. The US is the country with the highest incarceration rate in the world and its prisons on punishing its prisoners rather than rehabilitating them. The prisons often use drastic measures for isolating prisoners as a measure of control and do their best to strip them of their humanity. This may sound very barbaric, but what's worse is how similar it sounds to its school system.

"Losing touch with reality is me losing touch with being a human being. I don't want to make it seem like I have psychological problems but there's always that constant fear that is going to come after being here for so long. Everything you do is through these doors, these little holes (referring to

the hole pattern of his cell wall) and you'll notice that after we talk for a little bit that your vision will start to get distorted when you're looking at me through them like you have on those 3D glasses and this is how we spend our day. Now you could just imagine after 5, 10, 15 or 20 years of this you could imagine what it would do to one's mind. So, imagine a man sitting in a cage this size for 16 years, we're people as human beings who could fly people to the moon, and write the most beautiful poems we as human beings are so advanced, but we can't find a better way to assimilate people into society and to act correctly according to the laws instead of throwing them into cages and forgetting about them? I mean…it doesn't say much for who we are" [23]

- Anonymous inmate.

However, Joseph McGrath a Warden at the Pelican Bay suggests that because they have access to the inmate store, to buy "whatever they want" (from the limited options offered by the inmate store), twenty-four hours cable TV, and get visits he thinks inmates don't deserve these basic human necessities if they aren't going to evolve into model citizens. This is despite the fact that he is also against ideas on progressive rehabilitation and expects the inmates to instead evolve in their inhumane conditions. I don't know about you, but he sounds like a parent complaining about their child being spoiled and saying that they should earn these things without wanting to show them the right way. And just like in school, inmates and students are expected to know what the model behaviour is supposed to be without any encouragement. Pelican Bay is one of many prisons in the United States and it was built in the 1980s and the reason it is so tough on criminals is that the system still uses outdated methods that are no longer considered effective.

The three strikes law was created by Mike Reynolds after his daughter was taken away from him in a violent robbery. The way the system works is that a strike will be given to individuals who are convicted of a violent crime, and these "strikes" heavily worsen any future crimes committed by the individual. The biggest flaw in this system is it has caused many individuals to be incarcerated for life sentences for crimes such as theft or battery; making these crimes as severe as murder for any individual who already has a strike. Once a student reached their third strike with the teacher, he'd be sent to the principal's office who would then choose how to manage the situation. This is where the school system is different, as it still allows for the principal to decide the nuances of the situation; while in the prison system, it puts all violent crimes under the same umbrella without looking into the details of the crimes committed. The idea behind it is to make the law as simple yet as tough as possible because he says that if the convicted person is allowed to have so many chances, they should consider letting their victims have chances as well. People say that this is cruel since it creates human time bombs that will go off any second, but then you have other people who support this and say that there's no room for sympathy if you want to make society safe.

In Arizona, they're trying the same tough justice on less threatening criminals that are in for less than two years and for crimes such as not paying tickets. It was imposed by Joseph M. Arpaio, the sheriff of Phoenix, and he's openly against the education and rehabilitation of criminals. Instead of isolating them in cells, they walk in chain gangs in the streets doing community work to scare the population into telling their children that if they don't study, they'll end up like them. Similar to California, this system was made in the 1980s when crime rates began to increase, and the tolerance for crime was at a low point. Instead of solo confinement, they put them in tents and like a parent complaining about their child being spoiled, he disregards his inmates' discomfort and tells them that they're lucky to even have tents and cold sandwiches because it could be worst. Remember when I said that school leaves us confused when we get out? Well, depending on when someone who's serving a twenty-five-year prison sentence gets out, they are no longer prepared for the world they live in since the world and the people they knew are gone. When they do get out, they're going to have to rehabilitate themselves into the society that has changed. Like when you need to educate your grandparent or anyone above the age of sixty to use any smart device since they grew up with smart people and "not so smart" devices not the other way around.

In Helsinki, Finland, the prison system, just like their schooling system, is very different from any other country: not only is their justice system very humane, but Finland is also the world leader in keeping people out of jail. Before the 1960s, Finland had the highest imprisonment rate but then decided to cut down the sentences and focus its resources on rehabilitation. The success of this system is simple: the national prison director of Finland explains that the system is meant to display equity across the population by making fines proportional to their income.

The same thing is done through taxes for wealthier individuals, which allows these prisons to have the funding and resources necessary for individuals to be properly rehabilitated and productive for their society. This is a similar concept to how private schools are banned in the country so the wealthy must place their investments in education as a whole if they want their children's education to be of a decent quality. Therefore, whoever commits a crime will pay the fine and depending on the amount they make, a rich criminal will pay a bigger fine than a poor criminal for the same offence. Also, to imitate society, they have men and women in the same environment, to prevent stigmatization towards the other gender in the future. Unlike the US, which is tougher on kids, here in Finland people under the age of twenty-one don't go to jail, and adults who do time, rarely serve more than four years.

In the Finnish city of Vantaa, their higher security prisons may be well guarded, but their focus is still on rehabilitation. According to the inmates, having a massage in jail allows the energy of the people to reflect on the criminals and they learn to trust each other. For incarcerated women in Finland, any inmate who has an infant is allowed to have them stay together in the prison until the child turns five. This allows the children to keep their bond with their mother during infancy and nourishes the child's development. This is a very big development in the system in North America, which cuts the connection between parent and child to about four hours a day if someone is there to allow them to visit. For example, there's a testimony that says one of the female inmates was pregnant before getting arrested for drug trafficking, so they sent her to a rehab center, and she got clear but she also deserved to be in a "motherly prison center" where she got to give birth to her child and spend time with it. Just like the schools in Finland, these centers are forming mothers to be part of society with a contrastive tactic for rehabilitation. They don't focus on punishing the criminal, which just adds unnecessary pain to the crime committed; instead, Finland chooses to focus to make sure the crime doesn't happen again.

When you see the way the Finnish system does things, it's with a different psychology than the way we do things here. For example, just like my internship while doing time, you get some work experience the only difference is that the inmates get paid eight dollars per hour and pay for their expenses just like rent. The point of the American system is to gradually kill the killer from inside the person: we know that if a criminal has remorse for what he did, he will beat himself up for the rest of his life for his crime. But if you get them to gradually understand the reasons for their actions and take responsibility for them; they could then learn to love themselves and that's going to ease their shock when they return to society.

Do you remember in *Problem 1,* I quoted the minister of the Finish schools on why they've banned private schools and the message they want to send the kids about classism? And after that, I made the theory that you could apply the same logic to sexism, and this proves to be effective, as men and women who are placed in the same institute learn to interact with each other. Separation is supposed to prevent harm to the other sex in jails, but all it does is worsen the problem when the inmates get out. Since let's be real, once you get out into the world you need to learn how to interact with both sexes with far less restrictions. And that's why Krisa Tommy Moiland, the warden of the prison system, says *"Having both men and women helps have a nicer atmosphere, people want to take care of themselves, they want to comb their hair and look ok more than usual. I would be worried about some of the ideas that men have about women after spending years and years in a male-only prison, how would they behave and act in a normal setting where you will be meeting both sexes"* [24] Now the same way Finland fights classism by removing the concept of a private school and having all kids go to the same schools; it has also shown itself to be good at fighting sexism by having men and women in the same institute to learn how to take care of one another.

The goal of this rehabilitation is to kill the criminal within the person and not the other way around. Finland thinks that a human is innately good and acquires evil as it lives its life, so by stripping away evil with good things, the human naturally gravitates to its innate behaviour and participates in society. Look at it this way, if you break your leg and you could no longer walk, would they throw you in Timbuctoo and leave you there because you could no longer serve as a person in society? No, you'll get the help you need from the hospital and once you're better they'll gradually return you to society, and they treat prison time the same way. Since every jail sentence has a period (pun intended) and once that has been served, the inmates get out and slowly been prepared to live in society with the proper rehabilitation. That's why inmates in prison also can serve shorter sentences, since they are more likely to be prepared to return to society, they are also more likely to be released early on good behaviour.

As the popular saying goes, *"When Canada catches a cold, the US sneezes,"* because American-style prison systems have been implicated throughout Canada, like the Kingston Penitentiary in Toronto. The prison system in Canada is trying to replicate the tough justice system in the US by gradually stretching the sentences of the prisoners.

However, at the same time, Canada is trying to implicate curing criminals since it's more effective for treatment. But their problem is it's also less common for people to think of treating prisoners the Finnish way over here, so we are more easily influenced by the American way instead and that doesn't work since most of them only have a grade 8 education and grew up in abusive homes.

Consequently, in order to "cure" (rehabilitate) the criminals, they participate in cognitive skills such as problem-solving and dealing with anger and other emotions. Just like Finland, Canada's prison system goes from high-level maximum-security prisons with no freedom to minimum-security prisons that offer a lot of freedom for the inmates. The prison system allows many inmates the chance to go to lower security level prisons as they demonstrate good behaviour. Like Uncle Ben from *Spiderman* said, *"With great power comes great responsibility,"* and so as the inmate's prison system goes down in the security level, their level of personal responsibility rises. Therefore, like Finland's prison, the inmates in Canada under the minimal security prison system have apartments and know what chores they must do to maintain them. As an example, Jeff is an inmate who engaged in street gangs while he was a teenager. He says: *"I took a man's life; I threw him over a bridge during a robbery. I was 18 and I was disruptive, reckless, and arrogant. It was very unfortunate and tragic circumstances of course I chose to be there at that time, so I did what I did so here I am."* [25] And since his minimum-security prison exists on a farm, it allows Jeff to get a taste of freedom and gives him a sort of family since he raised some cows.

The Japanese way to function with prisons is pretty simple, just like their schooling system, it's centred on the community and shame. Therefore, if you respect the law, nothing bad will happen, but if you disobey there are strict punishments, and just like the US and the chain gangs there's a feeling of humiliation. The way that first-time offenders stay out of jail is that they need to feel remorse for their crimes, and the way they do it is that the criminals have to apologize to their victims, their families, and society; but if you get caught a second time for doing the same crime, they do the time for at least two years. They make their prisons military based to force a remodelling of their citizens into proper discipline. The Japanese prison system focuses on trying to push their inmates down the pass of the "model citizen" by giving them no other option when it comes to deviant behaviour.

This legal system reminds me of my high school, especially between classes since there's no one to force you to not go to class but there are consequences overall if you don't listen. If you don't go to your class after a few times, it looks bad on you, your parents, the school, and the school's reputation. Well, guess what? Just like in school, in the prison system in Japan, if the inmates are working and want to go somewhere, they need to raise their hand. I don't know about you but that can be pretty humiliating especially if you're trying to understand a certain topic, you need to voice your problems in front of everyone. For example, what if you need to go to the bathroom? In my personal experience even though I would often need to go during class, the teacher would force me every time to raise my hand in front of everyone, and every time I found it humiliating and annoying. They function as if they tried to install that on purpose, so raising your hand in class could install some nervousness to try to push you to not raise your hand or voice your opinion.

Thanks to its simple approach, Japan has one of the lowest crime rates in the world; and that's because its justice system focuses on community and conformity to shame offenders instead of sending them away. One special part of their justice system is called Kaminarimon Koban, where a "Koban" officer takes care of everything regarding a small area and acts as a one-man neighbourhood watch. Throughout Japan, there are about seven thousand Koban officers, and they are expected to visit twice a year every resident of their area to manage any legal or sometimes personal affairs. This reminds me of how at school, every time there is a new principal, they take the time to visit each class to meet and to get to know the kids and teachers. What I find interesting is that Koban officers are more effective at talking to citizens in his area, as he is already a part of the community and has a deeper understanding of people in the area than an outsider. He's informed about the latest neighbourhood gossip and does so to quickly identify who could be a potential troublemaker and stop them before they can commit a crime. This is just like a principal, who will typically go and meet with students who cause trouble instead of involving the police for problems associated with school property. Even Japan's main prosecutor isn't too interested in the idea of putting people in jail since his job is to keep people out.

I want to conclude with a saying I've previously said in this book, *"Life is the hardest exam because we try to cheat on each other not realizing we have different questions."* Since it's full of unexpected events and there's no way you could have seen it coming. Unlike your usual tests in class, where you get a study guide, time to study, and then have to go through it on your own. With life there's no study guide, the only way to ace the life test is by doing it together, sailing side by side with those you trust, so that you can ask them for help while still deciding on your own where you end up. And finally, the biggest thing that school and any form of prison have in common: it's confusing and time-consuming. Because we can see how confusing it all is just by seeing the reaction of an inmate or a student when they are asked what they are going to do when they go out: they have no clue; mostly because no one's prepared them for the outside world.

Problem 3

Outdated Learning System

The schooling system makes every child learn the same things in the same manner, and this method of teaching isn't authentic since they have to take a test, not to see if they understood the subject, it's to calculate how much of it has been memorized. The consequence of that, is as I mentioned in *Problem 1*: it puts a lot of pressure on students into thinking that they need to pass a standardized test not to be a disappointment. I mean take me for example, I've failed many tests, but this did not stop me from pushing forward and getting my degree; I knew what I wanted and didn't stop trying just because a class I didn't like told me *'I wasn't good enough.'* In other words, just because you don't pass your geography, history, math, science, or any class, in general, doesn't mean you are a failure. Parents, have you ever taken your child's homework, looked at it and was completely confused as to what they were learning? Now think about us students knowing it's going to be on the test. As children take on a stressful test, they would like to have their parents there to support them, also if they don't meet your expectations as a parent, how could you tell them to be better while looking at a portion of what could be on a potential test which was the homework, when it came to comprehension you froze like an antelope in headlights?

Howard Gardner, an American developmental psychologist at Harvard University, found nine forms of intelligence; a concept which the school system disregards completely. Parents I'm talking to you: Why is it that when you ask your children what they learn in school at the end of the day, their most common response is 'nothing much'? Well obviously, there's more than one problem here, but the point is the students don't feel like they've learned something useful; instead, it's something they need to learn just because it's going to be on a test, and once it's over they'll forget all about it. According to Hermann Ebbinghaus, a German psychologist who came up with the learning curve in 1880, there's a lap of time where you will forget things you've recently learned[26]. So of course, if there is an exam coming up you can only retain so much information compared to the amount of time you have to prepare. My eighth-grade

---

[26] Cunff, A. The forgetting curve: the science of how fast we forget. Ness Labs. April 22nd, 2022.

teacher's solution to the problem was to create a system showing us exactly what we had to study so that we could gauge what we had to do and more effectively manage our time accordingly.

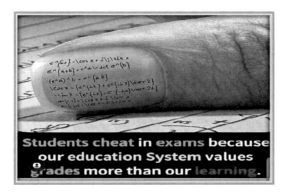

Do you know why students cheat? What does that mean when they do? It means that students don't have the time or resources needed to fully understand the subject that they've been taught for a test. And sadly, as students they feel pressured to excel in given tests even when they aren't prepared: our parents, our schools, and ourselves, pressure us into wanting to succeed no matter what, and that will result in finding methods to cheat.

Another reason some of us tend to cheat is due to the fact that on test day we either won't remember everything or as soon as they step out of the test room, they will forget it. This is due to the seven sins of the mind by Daniel Schacter, a professor of psychology at Harvard, he calls the first three 'sins of omission' which include forgetting important things: Transience, Absent-mindedness, or Blocking. According to

Dr. Schacter, these sins of omission come from failing to remember an idea, a fact, or an event (memory recovery). Among them, we have transience (general deterioration of a specific memory over time), absent-mindedness (attention failures that lead to memory loss) and blocking (inability to retrieve information.) [27] Transience plays with the learning curve, meaning that you'll forget the number of days between the teacher assigning you the test and the test day, your mind will just transient into it (pun intended). When it comes to absent-mindedness, it's just a question of not studying for too long or not knowing what to study, therefore the importance of a study guide. Because depending on how long you could stay effectively focused on one single task, at a point you'll either get distracted from the outside noise or the racing thoughts inside your head about the test and that will lead you to not stay as focused. Sadly, you got the last one and that's a blockage, when you are sitting there trying to figure out that one problem, you know it's on the tip of your tongue, or should I say pencil? (pun intended) but the stress is what's preventing you from writing it down. Overall, these three sins prevent most students from passing their tests with the grade they wanted which could result in low self-esteem.

I understand, for most teachers or parents it can be embarrassing if you read a book and it shows where all the students from a certain grade are supposed to be, what notions

---

[27] Schacter, D., 2020. Daniel Schacter's Seven Sins of Memory. Exploring your mind. November 28th 2021.

they should have, and where should they be. I also understand it can make you feel bad if your students don't perform as well since it looks bad on you and the school. Another funny thing that brings both these systems together is that the more we find methods to cheat, the more we penalize those who have good intentions. For example, a student who doesn't cheat is still forced to leave his phone in his locker before a test, move away from anyone he knows, and is restricted from going to the bathroom; all measures are used to try to prevent the one kid who is cheating in class. It's simple, be real with yourself and your students while you're creating the exams; have the students take out their binders, and you take out your book and go over what you actually taught them, to evaluate how ready they are for their test. As a teacher, you should go through all the student's binders to make sure they are all up to par with the test content and any students who are lacking need extra support. Students will feel better that they're being evaluated on things they know, and you can assure that all your students will be at their best since what they know should be a mirror reflection of your test.

The school also stigmatizes jobs that they consider to be of 'lower quality,' like taxi drivers, garbage men, or fast-food operators. Then, they use that stigma to alarm children into believing that if they don't study hard enough or get into the right schools they will end up like those people. They also condemned any jobs related to arts because they are viewed as "not very high paying" or "too risky." With that being said, the jobs that many people view as high paying and successful are doctors, lawyers, judges, etc. While these jobs do pay well, it is still important to remember that these other jobs are just as important. All of these jobs are just as important to make our society function, and it's wrong that schools push people to look down on some of them simply because they require different or 'manual' skills. but if your definition of success is that linear path, then you need to redefine your view of success. As the popular saying goes *"Don't put all your eggs in one basket."*

Let's put all this research aside for a minute and take me for example. I remember when I needed to study for math, science, or anything that I considered useless; I would go home and open up my exercise book to review my notes, but I felt as if I were reading gibberish. However, at school, I would comprehend the exercises and I wasn't afraid to raise my hand to answer a question. The reason I could do this is because it's all happening at the moment, so there's little time to forget what's been taught. All your students are different and want to achieve different things in life, so not everyone will retain the same information the same way. It's also important to remember that not all students learn things at the same pace, but that doesn't mean they are less interested in the subject. I remember throughout high school I was one of the only students who raised their hand to talk, or I wouldn't wait until the teacher is done talking before raising my hand to answer the question. Get this, there's no A in the word school but there's one in the word learning and memorization. In other words, if teachers and parents really want students to get all A's, they should consider teaching the subject in a way that's more dynamic to fit the student's learning style.

Teachers, I'm talking to you, support the students as if they are oranges in a wheelbarrow, and you're a delivery person. If an orange falls off, you can't call it a pet because it will roll in the wrong direction. Instead, it's best to stop the wheelbarrow and go grab the lonely orange. Now at this point you know that I am comparing students to oranges in a wheelbarrow because they don't have control over their education, the teacher does, and that is why he is the delivery person, in control of the movement of the wheelbarrow, which is the class and the speed by which students are learning. If the delivery person goes too fast an orange is going to fall, similar to a student either losing the class and becoming confused or losing interest and wandering off doing other things. In either one of those cases, the teacher should stop the lesson for maybe a few days, talk to the child in question, and help them get back on board. Trust me, it can't hurt anyone because the rest of the students will have time to do other things, like revise what they have learned previously while the struggling student will have one on one time with the teacher which can improve that child's comprehension. And teachers, don't say that "*we can't do anything about it because it's the curriculum and we have to follow it.*" The policymakers just assumed that it'll take this amount of time to teach this subject to a class of this many people, without even learning it for themselves, or stepping into a student's shoes.

The policy makers have made assumptions on the curriculum but it's the teachers' job to make sure the child understands. If we go back to my wheelbarrow metaphor and we say that the curriculum is the journey that the wheelbarrow must make it to the end with all the oranges aboard, the policymakers have only assigned the road and said, *"You have to finish the class in this amount of time, and make sure there are a certain number of tests to grade the students."*

And if the teacher replies, *"What if the class takes longer?"* Then the policymaker says, *"You shouldn't need more time for what you're covering. If the students need more time, they should learn to learn faster! Give them more homework, it'll make them used to the pace of the class."*

As the Russian proverb goes, *"The boiling water that softens the potato, will harden the egg."*

Different people will react in diverse ways to the same environment. When you put one kid under pressure, they might thrive and work twice as hard; but another may panic and start to fail the class as a result. Therefore, it's unfair to expect the same answer from both of them when one thrives and the other one is trying to survive. What makes a school year hard isn't the amount of classes you have, it's the amount of content you have for the classes and not enough time to do it. The problem is that the policymakers make the curriculum for each subject but are not the ones to teach it. That tells us that they don't understand how long it takes to teach the concepts they want students to learn. They make it a quantity-over-quality scenario, where only half the class is absorbed for a crammed subject instead of the whole content being comprehended for a lighter course load. Because every student learns at a different pace it could even be good to add different densities of curriculum for different students who work at different paces but set it up for the contents to be the same.

Do you remember the so-called work/life balance I mentioned in the section *Problem 1: School vs. Jobs?* The four burners theory explains that we only have so much energy to spend on everything in our life: health, friends, and family. If we spend more time on work, naturally we'll have to take time and energy from one of the other three *'Burners'* to give it more attention. Well, when we look at our classes in a semester at school it's the same thing. Since the thing is just like that balance, you're supposed to have between all the great aspects of your life, you have to make sure that you're not falling behind in any of your classes. The problem is just like with work, you can't keep your energy at maximum for every subject every time, since by doing so, you'll burn yourself out. Everyone has that one subject in school that's going to click with you naturally, and one that you won't understand for the life of you. So, by default, you'll spend more time on the one that comes to you easily since it brings you joy, while the other will take the back burner. Take me and math for example, when I would fail a test, I wouldn't tell myself "It's okay you'll get it next time," because I'd be lying to myself since I'm already bad and that test result just proves my point. Since the odds of me getting a good grade in math is much smaller than me getting a good grade in psychology even if I'd spend more time studying for math than psychology it wasn't going to end up helping me with the test. I understand that not everyone thinks this way and that's okay since I only developed that thought pattern when I realized that in the journey to obtain the average result, I would have to work twice as hard and still not be satisfied. Therefore, when I realized that studying for a psychology test would get me a better result and make me happier than trying to work twice as hard but get a half result in math.

When I was in ninth grade, my teacher for geography left halfway through the semester very suddenly, and no one knew why. He left for weeks on end, and of course, we didn't learn what we were supposed to at that time, and we still had an exam to pass. As the days turned into weeks, we had supply teachers that would stay for a couple of days with plans to teach us some things, and some would come with nothing and expect us to work we were never given. After a while, our class started to mentally fall apart, some became anxious because there was no teacher, and some were happy because they could just fool around. However, two months before our exam, we had a permanent substitute who came as a replacement and completely changed our ballgame. Since it was so close to the end of the semester, and we had so much to do, we quickly encountered two big problems regarding the class.

First of all, we were exhausted of all the replacement teachers that came in, so we didn't take things seriously and she had to find a way to get us all on board. Second, since we didn't learn much material throughout the semester, she had to cram all the information that we didn't get to learn in a small window of time. I honestly don't remember if she was able to modify the exam, or if it was already finalized and she somehow managed to get it all through to us.

My first teacher that left taught me a study method that I'll never forget, and that's how he would teach his classes. It's called the Pomodoro technique, and I remember on the first day of school he told us that our brains can actively focus on something for at least twenty to thirty minutes and then our brains would start losing their focus from there. At first, we complained about how it wasn't fair that he had ten times more teaching time than we had of break time; but he explained how if you get a break longer than that, your brain gets used to what you're doing and completely let's go of what you were taking a break from. He even explained to us that's why commercials are a maximum of two minutes long and that they are intervallic between the twenty-to-thirty-minute length of a regular show's runtime. They do that because they know your brain will try and find something else to entertain itself with after that period of time. However, they keep the ads short to have your full attention, since when you switch activities, your brain is at its peak of focus, which will also stop you from wanting to click off the program. This same tactic is just as effective when you use it to learn new things, as your brain will spend the first half hour absorbing the most knowledge before it needs to be refreshed by switching topics.

My teacher was also one of those rare teachers who knew students actually had lives outside of school, much like the teachers themselves. For this reason, during that two-minute break, you'd be able to ask him about your homework for that night, and then he'd show you how to do it, so you'd get it done on the spot. Looking back to the class restrictions we talked about in *Problem 1*; well during that two-minute break he'd remove all of them, he'd let us get up, stretch, talk to our friends, go on our phone, rest our eyes, you name it. Because all he asked of us was twenty minutes of our full attention, and in return, he would give us two minutes to unwind.

Another class that helped me navigate high school and my workload was my "self-management" class. The goal of the course was to find strategies that worked for you throughout different exercises. For example, the teacher taught us how to effectively use our agendas or planners on our computers such as Google calendars, or organize our desktop with folders etc. We got little homework and if you finish the work that was assigned for the day, he highly recommends that you get unfinished things from other classes to work on. The teacher also taught French, English, History, Geography, and Math, so you could ask him questions related to any of those subjects for your work and he'd do his best to help you. This class allowed us to optimize our time and was the best course to have in the last period as it liberated us from any other homework that we were given earlier in the day.

Here's a trick for students: when you're learning something for the first time the idea is to break it down. Since we didn't have a teacher for so long, and nobody took the class seriously, we slacked off. That meant we had to learn a lot of things in a short amount of time, and even then, the amount of effort people were putting into the class was too low to have influence. Hermann Ebbinghaus's experiment concluded *"Repeated learning sessions over a longer interval of time improves memory retention on any subject"*[28]; that was the opposite in my case, I had a lot to learn in a brief period of time.

In conclusion, the education system still uses old methods of teaching their students that favour a quantity of content over the quality of what's retained. This makes the education system inauthentic as the students don't become more educated in learning, they just learn to pass tests that satisfy the dated system. You could add or modify classes, but they can't be removed since it's supposed to prepare students for what's to come next year.

The tests we do are made to exercise our short-term memory, and these exams are too far for most of that content to be still remembered. But exams don't help improve the long-term memory of the content for the student either, it just forces the students to do every test over again at once. On top

[28] "Hermann Ebbinghaus." AZQuotes.com. Wind and Fly LTD, 2021. April 6th, 2021.

of that, most of the time the modules teachers teach you don't add up, so combining them isn't the best way to go.

For example, in eleventh grade I had an intro to Psychology, Anthropology and Sociology where we only spend a little amount of time covering each subject, I didn't like this simply because I loved psychology and I wished we had spent more time on it from the start to actually understand the subject and they are all about human behaviour. Also, not to mention that when you switch modules in class that the previous module doesn't prepare you for the next, it's harder to see where every piece of information fit in.

When we talk about Psychology, we're talking about someone's well-being and the train of thought behind how a person feels and interacts with the world and the people around them and that shapes their personality. When we talk about Sociology, we're talking about how individuals could come together with their view of the world and create what we know as a society or a community and the rules of how to live in one. And finally, when we talk about Anthropology, we're talking about culture, rituals, celebrations, religion, and anything that differentiates one group of people from another. If the goal is to teach everything there's to teach about that subject to then leave it behind, then my suggestion is to teach one every year and for the twelfth grade you get to choose which one you like. But if you want to show how they all come together, you need to instruct the students knowing that each person has a unique brain chemistry, that will influence their feeling, perceptions, interactions and their personality and their psychology. Then you bring two or more people together and they have to create something that they all are going to benefit from and from that, ensure their survival and that is what you call society, community, and sociology. After a while people just start doing things and since it helps us survive or brings us some sense of purpose then that's a beginning of a ritual when it's repeated generation after generation it becomes a culture known to a particular group of people and that's where you get anthropology. The way I see it, that doesn't make sense because it's very counterintuitive; the reason you spend a month minimum on every sub-module to better understand the module, then you have a test on that specific concept to be able to put it behind you since you need to move on and tackle the next subject.

Here's another example with science, especially physics could get complicated so my friend Pierce said it best, *"Physics is the combination of math and science, where the real world can be broken down into mathematical values."* Because physics can be really hard to explain to people who don't understand it, he believes the best way to teach it is to make people connect with what the values mean. For example, three values in physics that are used a lot are time (seconds), mass (kilograms), and distance (meters). To explain how these values relate to each other, he gave me the example of a moving car; the speed that the car travels is how much time it takes for the car to move a certain distance, and the amount of energy that the car needs to move depends on the car's mass.

Teachers let's be real for a minute, if you would put everything you taught your students in the final exam, it would be longer than a couple of pages and it would take way more than a couple of hours to complete. In other words, you can't put everything, only the essentials; but then what's the point to learn all those extra things if you bring us back to basics? If you take each module at a time since they are subjects of their own. Don't bother giving an 'end of the year' exam that covers everything, just focus on the 'end of the module' exam. Think of it, everyone wins in this situation, you only need to teach a subject once and your students can focus more intensely on one portion of the course at a time instead of just skimming over the highlights. You also won't have to spend your time creating an end-of-the-year exam, and your students won't have to stress over it. Here's my advice, with each 'end of module' exam, look at the modules with the lowest scores. Those are the portions of the class that clearly need more understanding, and would therefore require more time, and a second test to improve the understanding of the class.

Okay, take it from me, throughout high school, I had exams that would jeopardize my math by a lot to the point that I failed my ninth and eleventh-grade math classes. This was because every math exam forced me to try to remember everything from a semester in, which I only had a surface-level understanding. It would have been better for the teacher to take more time in each lesson to get students to understand each concept, and then evaluate us on it to make sure we understood; and if the grades of the test were low, then surely, we didn't and needed more time on the subject. Since what gave me a hard time was the fact that I had to backtrack everything I learned from day one, under lots of pressure and in a short amount of time. Here's the thing, your students aren't learning anything when it's taught under the pressure of strict deadlines; do you remember my mess up in geography class? Although the new teacher did help the class pass the exam, I don't remember anything she taught because it was all taught to us in such a rush.

Homework should serve one purpose, and that is to provide extra practice to help you absorb what you've learned, but first, you need to make sure that the student understands the subject. To evaluate your student's comprehension, to see if they are ready to do homework on their own, you should give them all work in class that you go through together. This will allow you to see which students are struggling with the material and will make sure that they can actually do the homework you give them. There is no "appropriate" age to tell a child something if you're creative enough you could find a way to explain anything to them without getting them confused. As Albert Einstein once said, *"If you can't explain it simply, you don't understand it well enough."* [29]

The biggest problem with the school system is that you teach your students with books, base their tests off those same

[29] A-Z Quotes. 2021. *Albert Einstein Quote*. June 24th, 2021.

books and grade them for how much they can retain of what you taught them from that book. That's fine… to establish the basics, but then you need to add onto the student's lessons with what's outside the book: enrich your students by explaining your understanding of the subject matter. Now of course I understand that you can't change the math equations, historical facts, scientific facts, and other things that are well-established because those things are essential. However, if your student doesn't understand these fundamental concepts and is getting bad grades in these classes, you need to teach them uniquely. You should teach the children how to use those equations, facts, and experiments elsewhere than on a test. For example, finances use math, and we need it to manage our money; algebra can teach us how to estimate costs and any other quantities in day-to-day life. Let's say we're paying for gas, and the price of gas is \$1.59 per litre. Then if X is the number of litres, you put in, Y becomes the value you'll have to pay. So now you have the equation $Y = 1.59(X)$ which can help you gauge either how much money you'll need to fill up the car (like if it's 20 litres, you'll be paying \$31.80), or you can use it to know how many litres a certain amount of money can get you (like \$20 will get you 12.6 litres of gas).

Kurt Lewin, a German American psychologist, once said *"You can't understand something until you try to change it* ''[30]. Therefore, history can be interesting since it can serve to change something that's there by learning how it worked in the past or its origin. History is a vast topic, there isn't just a simple "history class" for the entire world, it is usually history focusing on a specific place and at a specific time. I would like to make this small yet essential distinction, if you want to speak on a topic, you must make sure that you know about it entirely before wanting to critique it. For example, if you were to study someone's life, you would have to study their psychology before and after each big event in their life to fully understand what the event's short-term and long-term effects are on said person. Or, in the case of changing the school system, you would have to go back in its history to see where the roots of its problems lie, and what can be done to improve it.

You can't drill information in a student's head because it will screw them up (pun intended). You also can't program them to be the best from the get-go as that comes with trial and error, just like programming Artificial Intelligence (AI) to do a certain task with efficacy. Instead of having students think they're failures, you should give them the chance to bounce back from a setback. You can never know what that child is facing, on top of having to deal with you belittling them, since there's always room for improvement. With the constant belittlement from teachers and comparison with their

---

[30] TOP 13 QUOTES BY KURT LEWIN | A-Z Quotes. A-Z Quotes. August 12th 2022,

parents, that student could develop a cognitive distortion called "overgeneralization" since it will play on their self-esteem. That's when you assume that you'll fail whatever it is your doing after one try. On top of that, you put into students' heads that it will impact their future as if being unable to solve an eleventh-grade algebra question will stop them from making it as a film producer. What I'm getting at is this letter from the principal in Singapore she wrote a letter telling the parents that even if their children don't pass a test, it doesn't make them unworthy of their parent's love.

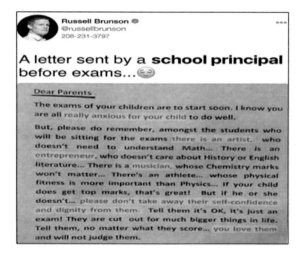

Now regardless of if it's true or not, why do you need that confirmation to apply it for yourself? Since learning doesn't stop with school, if we were taught how to think and not what to think we'd be less confused about our place in society once we graduated. What I mean is, you've been asked multiple times what you wanted to be, and after high school, you are either lucky, and continue following that initial path, or you end up changing interests and feel a bit lost and confused in the post-secondary world. The reason you're lost is because once you're out of high school you realize what you've been taught isn't what you need to know to navigate the sea of life. In other words, don't let the grades block you from learning outside of school.

The question throughout this whole book was what the use of school is. Well, I think that it's a great place to see your friends and make new ones. Because, unlike homeschooling, you have to not only invest in your child's education plan, but you need to make sure they get to have fun by putting them in camps if they like it, and that can be easier said than done. In addition, for the parents who want to homeschool their kids properly, they would have to not only be invested in their children's education but also put money aside for certain things such as the internet, taxes, tutors and from a legal standpoint you have to make sure that the curriculum that you want to teach your child is appropriate according to the minister of education.[31] Because there are parents that don't have time for their children's education so they send them to school. But, if it's for educational purposes school can be useless, and the reason is because these days you can learn anything on the internet and you have everyday life to learn from.

[31] Kaminski, J. How Much Does Homeschooling Cost to Educate Your Child - Brighterly. June 14th 2022,

If I were to give an opinion, I would say that the school system has failed to prepare children for the responsibilities of being an adult. And to give a solution to this problem, there are a couple of things that school should teach us: capitalism, the study of oneself, how to sustain good relationships with healthy boundaries, and everyday life skills. The reason for capitalism is simple if your county operates under a capitalistic system, you should be educated on how money works and how to spend it. To properly understand the economy, we don't need all the extreme math we use in school either. Like the gas example above, most transactions with money can be calculated with the knowledge of arithmetic. A good education in economics can help with many parts of the capitalist world, like filling taxes, understanding the stock market, how to apply for a loan from a bank, the difference between a good or a bad debt, what is a credit score and what is its purpose; and this barely scratches the surface.

To start things off, a good debt is an investment that generates value for you in the long term, you could invest in multiple aspects of your life. However, bad debt is when you buy something, that's not necessary, at a high-interest rate and you're not able to pay it back in time and in its entirety. A credit card is a card that has money with a certain limit and that money belongs to the bank. When you buy things with your card, you have one month to pay the credit statement if you don't, that's when interests come into play, and depending on the rate, things get interesting (pun intended). The more you use your credit card and the more you get into the habit of paying it back, the better your credit score will be and the more the bank will trust you and your limit could increase. And the better your credit score, you could apply for a loan for a house, car, etc.

You also can't properly teach about the economy without talking teaching us about budgeting; just like how teachers give us so much homework yet fail to teach us time management, you're given money without any knowledge about how to manage it. It's the same thing, they want us to get into the best schools, to have the best jobs, for us to lead successful lives, however, fail to teach us how to manage our money. And think of it, teaching children how to manage money will not only make them more responsible but might make them more empathetic towards their parents when they can't buy them something. If you're a teacher and you don't know where to start, I suggest the key points of the book "*rich dad, poor dad*[32]" by Robert Kiyosaki. The importance of teaching economics is to give students an understanding of the value of money because just like time, it's often misused and taken for granted.

When it comes to post-secondary education, in most cases you'll have to pay a tuition fee; and depending on your situation the price can vary greatly. For example, when it came to my, tuition fees for my two-year college program total came up to $5842. Luckily for me, my parents were able

[32] YouTube, Escaping the ordinary (BC Marx) ,"rich dad, poor dad", February 2nd, 2021,

to help, and as a Canadian resident living close by, tuition was the only payment to worry about. However, the system couldn't resist making money off people who don't understand it in the first place, meaning when it comes to students who've immigrated to study abroad, they had to pay a lot more than me. I have a friend I've met throughout college and she's in the opposite situation as I am. She's a foreign student who lives alone, and she's in the same two-year program as I am, but she pays a total of $28,490 on top of having to pay for her life here in Canada. And let me remind you of something, because we studied during the COVID-19 pandemic, we spent the majority of it in front of a screen only going on campus once a week during our second year; meaning at least half of that money could have been used for other things such as rent in her case. And this ties into what I talked about in *Problem 1* and *Problem 4* because I mentioned that if your parents immigrated here and they realize that since you become a foreign student when it comes to college it's more expensive. Normally, if her parents were paying for her education, in return her parent would want her to be at the top of her class. The problem with this is it sets an unfair standard for the student, who is put under pressure to succeed and of having to justify their education. Money managing and time management are equally important; as we use our time to make money, so badly spending money is also badly spending your time as well. The reason parents push their children to have a high education and a high-paying job is that we all know that we can't make more time, so they make up for it by wanting you to make more money instead.

Money management can also help us understand how to develop a proper relationship with money. Many people take money for granted and spend it as soon as they get it, while others take it too seriously and keep it all to themselves. In both these cases, an unhealthy relationship with money can lead to a miserable life, which is why its value needs to be understood when we're still young and the concept of money is still new. Having too much money could make you behave in three ways, which I will call the three S ($$$) inspired by Jay Shetty's book *'Think Like a Monk'*:

- Selfish "I want more money": They will find ways to always make more money, they might also be the ones who chase those high-paying jobs or turn to inventing things to make money.
- Sufficiency "I have what I need to get by": They don't feel the need to have everything, they understand the difference between needs and wants.
- Service "I want more to give more": They will find ways to make money, but the difference is that they want to give back.

My parents used to teach me and my siblings that when you earn money there is a portion you can spend now, a portion that you save up to spend later (usually for a special thing to buy on a special occasion), and money that you save up for when you retire. I started learning about money management at ten years old. My mom and I were in the kitchen, and she made me dump all my money on the table to count it up, and the total was about $150. With that money, she told me to divide it into three groups: the spending now, then saving up for something special, and the retirement fund; the ratio was 50%, 25% and 25%. Half would go in the "spending now" group, and she said that it's the biggest because it's for all your expenses such as food, gas, rent, and basic pocket money used for everyday life.

The first twenty-five percent was in the category of "save up for something special", and she said that by starting to save up for it now, you'll be able to afford it when you need it. It's smaller since it's something that you can save up for over time such as a car, a special gift for someone, or just a big purchase for yourself; you'll appreciate whatever you use it on even more too because of the effort it took to wait before you buy it. I remember the first thing I bought myself was a black Canon camera with a sixty-four-gigabit memory card, and I bought it because at the time I loved taking pictures. It was a little passion for me, so buying it after saving up for it felt amazing. Later on, when college came around, I also saved up for an Acer laptop and at the beginning I was going to use it for taking notes during in-person college, and now since school is online it became my lifeline to school.

The last twenty-five percent is for retirement and the reason for that is because you don't work forever, and there's a point where you need to simply relax and enjoy life. Think of it as building a bed, the more you build it, the more you'll get tired, and want to just collapse and sleep; but you can't do that if there's no bed, can you? It was on my tenth birthday that I learned about the money we put into a retirement fund, and on that day my grandma gave me a hundred dollars in ten-dollar bills, which was the first money placed into my newly opened bank account. All this to say, budgeting is important because it's something you can do to make sure that you'll be happy in the future; just like time management allows for you to make the best out of the present moment.

Jack Kornfield said, "*In life, only three things matter: how well we lived; how well we loved and how well we learned...to let go.*"[33] Therefore, you must do all these things that are essential while remembering that you have an expiry date, the thing is none of us know exactly when that expiry date is. The point here is that both time and money management are important, and once you get out of school, you'll need to manage them both on your own; so why not start now?

Another thing that schools should teach students is how to be introspective, which means how to understand yourself and how to accurately assess a situation. Because if academic tests are supposed to evaluate your knowledge of a certain subject, then you should be able to study yourself just like any subject to be prepared for all life situations. Let me tell you

---

[33] A-Z Quotes. 2021. *Jack Kornfield Quotes About Letting Go | A-Z Quotes.* June 16th, 2021.

that in every class I've had in college so far, the first unit of learning has been on me. As in, what type of person I am, and what I want from social work. In the same way, you get prepared for tests so you can nail them, the sooner you can identify what you want and when you'll be able to have enough self-control to get through tough situations. And once you know yourself, you could identify what kind of jobs and friends you're suited for. Tyler Perry has a tree analogy saying that your friends are like parts of a tree. You have the leaves, the branches, and the roots, which describe the type of relationship you will have with those types of people.

An example of knowing yourself on an academic level is the self-management class I took in ninth grade, which was knowing ourselves on the school plan, knowing what studying tools worked for us, getting help with work from other classes etc. You find your reason a class like that should be mandatory. The last thing that should be in this new schooling system is establishing relationships and knowing how one's home life can affect their schooling, and vice versa. You should learn about forgiveness, kindness, and tips to manage anxiety; and these things should continue to be taught in high school because many people forget about them. I'm sure you've been anxious about a moment in your life and knowing how to deal with it can have a positive effect on how you live your day-to-day life. When it comes to forgiveness, think about it as an act for yourself since you no longer have to protect yourself from any emotional pain. I don't understand how people hold grudges, but I could understand why, it has to do whatever you've done to hurt someone else, and they aren't over it or just hold onto it just to find another reason to hate and hold it over your head.

Did you know that the word **PROPER** is composed of the three first letters of **pro**fessional and **per**sonal, but unlike the word itself if you look in the dictionary, you'll get the word personal before the word professional. Meaning that your personal life should come first to ensure that they're both balanced out because they both influence each other. As much as our profession might become a huge part of our life, we can't let it make us neglect our personal life. For example, if someone close to you dies, it's important to take a couple of days off to grieve for your loss, since the emotional baggage of grief will stop you from being able to properly function. This also works the other way around, I remember when I got fired from Canadian Tire, my manager gave me an option to either finish my day or go home; I wanted to go but I didn't know how my parents would react to me coming home so soon, so I worked that day, but it felt uneasy. What made matters worse was that both of my parents came to pick me up and asked me if I got my schedule for the holidays. I took a deep breath and told them "Merry Christmas, I got fired." To my surprise, they didn't react very harshly.

Joseph Sternberg explains the three aspects of good relationships through his triangle of love: Intimacy, Commitment, and Passion; and how the absence of one of these three elements could lead to an entirely different formation of a relationship, platonic or not. The aspect of intimacy can be expressed in four different forms [34]

- **Cognitive or Intellectual intimacy**: The act of sharing a deep and meaningful conversation with someone.
- **Experimental intimacy**: Doing a fun activity together, like playing a game.
- **Emotional intimacy**: Knowing how to be there for them and understanding their struggles by displaying empathy.
- **Sexual intimacy**: Sharing a good physical bond with someone, and that bond could become emotional in a romantic setting or can remain simply physical as well.

Sex is part of life, and proper sexual education could work wonders in understanding sexuality and maintaining a healthy sex life. In Canada, sexual education is mandatory in all of the ten provinces as well as the three territories.[35] The problem is that it's not the same everywhere, and here are some examples that they've said:

"To clarify the lack of consistency across the country, examples are listed below (from 2015), highlighting the two ends of the spectrum regarding age (other provinces fall between the two extremes).

[34] The Infidelity Recovery Institute. August 29th, 2017. *The Four Types of Intimacy - The Infidelity Recovery Institute*.
[35,37, 38] Arcc-cdac.ca. 2005. *Sex Education in Canada*.

- British Columbia and Manitoba require children to know the proper name for body parts in kindergarten, while PEI and New Brunswick wait until Grade six.
- Sexual orientation is taught in Ontario, Saskatchewan, and Nova Scotia in Grade three, but Newfoundland and Labrador only teach LGBT awareness in grade nine (Manitoba has no clear agenda.)
- Information about STIs and prevention is taught in Nova Scotia starting in Grade Five, but New Brunswick avoids the topic until Grade Ten.
- Birth Control is taught in Grade 6 in BC, and Grade nine in Nova Scotia and Saskatchewan. Nova Scotia teaches about STI prevention in Grade Five but waits until high school for birth control, and some provinces refuse to discuss gender identity and LGBT concerns at all."[36]

While it is a good thing that the provinces have done work to try to implement some form of sexual education across Canada, I think a curriculum regarding sexual education should be unified across the country. This would allow for a fair education on the subject for everyone no matter where they come from and would allow for the subject to be treated more seriously, I think basic anatomy, the proper names for body parts, and a basic understanding of consent should be taught in kindergarten like British Columbia and Manitoba *"No one should touch your body without you being okay with it."*

And the class shouldn't be divided by biological sex, since basic anatomy is useful for everyone, and consent is a huge concept that also applies to everyone. Once you get to middle school you review what you were taught in kindergarten, then you can add onto the topic of sexual anatomy with the effects of puberty, and how it changes you both physically and mentally. This should also be followed by discussing STDs and how to prevent them, discussing sexual orientation and LGBTQ2A+ awareness, and learning about the legal and social concept of consent[37]. In high school, you should revise everything that's been learned this far, and then teach things such as the harmful effects of pornography, sexual kinks, sexual positions, prostitution, and how your upbringing influences your sex life or sexual orientation. High school should also discuss how your mental health could affect your sex drive, and interpersonal relationships like ADHD, body dysmorphia, sleep apnea, or being addicted to sex can also affect your perception of sexual interactions.

This should be a mandatory class that everyone attends, and it should be taught every year in steps starting from basic anatomy for younger kids, and escalating to masturbation, puberty, and safe sex during high school. The goal should be for students to hopefully take these ideas and implement them in their lives. Another thing, when it comes to sex education in middle and high school, this should be the only class that is divided by biological gender. If you're a male, a male teacher should teach you, and if you're a girl, a female teacher should teach you. For students who are non-binary or transgender, they should be given the choice of which gender they wish to be placed in the class to allow them more comfort with their environment. I can only speak from personal experience: being taught my sexual education in my elementary school brought me a couple of benefits, you don't shy away from asking personal questions since there's privacy in what you're learning.

I do realize that learning about everything together and having the guys and the girls in one class and having both teachers there could have its benefits. However, to maximize comprehension and empathy, it would be good for students to learn about both sexes from their perspective. Essentially doing a teacher swap for the topic of opposite gender such as, the female students all together learn about the male sex from a male teacher and vice versa with the female teacher. For example, it is useful to learn about the other sex not only for pleasure but for understanding the function and effects of the sexual organ. For example, learning about erectile dysfunction, how come women have a fertility window but men do not, learning about how the body produces the main hormone for the appropriate sex, and why women get period cramps.

Let me tell you something teachers, you are your students' best tool for learning, since at home their parents are too busy or unwilling to take part in their child's education, and children do not have the resources to teach for themselves. When you allow your personal bias to slip into the curriculum by omitting parts of a class, it can remove its potential to teach children valuable information they could use for the rest of their lives. For example, the myth that women do not masturbate. Women's bodies have been historically dominated and examined by men, and Christianity believes that a woman should find a man to please her, instead of trying to sexually pleasure herself. This creates a system where the woman is forced to be dependent on a man for her to achieve any form of socially acceptable sexual pleasure and why is it a man's job to figure that out if it is the women's body? And because neither sex has been taught about the other's sexual organs, the man is pressured to try to sexually satisfy his sexual partner without understanding how sexual pleasure works on her end.

Let me ask you a question if you love preparing your students in every other subject so they feel at ease when the test arrives; why is it harder to give proper sex education in schools to make them feel at ease if and when they are going to have a romantic or sexual relationship? One thing that desperately needs awareness is being transgender; here's an example of a parent whose child came out as transgender and being transparent about her experiences[38]. According to her, you want to start with the definition of gender, which is an expression and an identity, whereas sex is determined by the genitalia between your legs and your pronouns associated with the gender which you identify with. Gender roles often describe the actions and clothing worn by people who are assigned to a biological gender, and being transgender simply means you identify more to the opposite gender from what you were born with. It is also important to understand the two types of transitions: Social, when you identify with your pronouns and introduce yourself as such to your social circle; and Surgical when you undergo a gender-altering surgery as well as hormone therapy treatment to allow you to biologically associate with the sex you identify with. Therefore, parents would need to educate themselves and their children about the concepts of sexuality and gender, so they can more effectively understand themselves and the people around them.

As a student, when you do not feel like you're being taught everything in class, you have a choice to either ask the teacher for more information or find out more about the subject elsewhere (like the internet, books, etc.) When dealing with sex education, however, it can be a bit awkward for students to ask the teacher questions (especially in front of their peers). The way the class is also taught is also completely

---

[38] Pullkett, T. *How to teach your kid what transgender means.* Today's parenting. June 14th, 2022,

dependent on the views of the curriculum and the teacher, making it difficult for students to get an evenly distributed education on the subject. If you think about it, this "monkey see monkey do logic" works perfectly when we put it onto children being exposed to hyper-sexual activity and taking it in without knowing better. This leads many sexually confused teenagers to adopt a monkey-see, monkey-do type of mentality, which oftentimes is not the healthiest approach. Many vulnerable teenagers tend to overcompensate because they consume hyper-sexualized media online, like porn, or hookup culture created by dating apps. Many other teenagers can go the other way and move away from sexual activity altogether if they were scared by hyper-sexualization, or if their parents are religiously conservative, they might have a preconceived idea of sex as a terrible thing.

In 1961 Albert Bandura a Canadian American psychologist at Stanford University conducted a three-step study experiment called "bobo-dolls"[39]. He wanted to see if the so-called monkey see monkey do apply to children, so he took a bunch of preschoolers and divided them into three study groups. The first one was exposed to adults mistreating the dolls, the second group was exposed to adults being nice to the dolls, and the third group was not exposed to any behaviour. Then they were divided by gender into subgroups who were watching either the same-sex model or opposite-

[39] Nolen, Jeannette L. "Bobo doll experiment". Encyclopedia Britannica, May 26th, 2020.

sex models. The conclusion that was observed was that the boys from the first group were observed to recreate the aggressive behavior, more than the girls from that same group. Given the fact that adults are showing how the dolls should be treated to children who do not know better, then you could see how that pattern could repeat itself with young teenagers.

I understand that when the internet was not a thing, a school's primary job was to teach kids a basic education and take care of them while their parents were at work. Although the internet can be a double-edged sword, it can be a particularly useful tool for students to learn things beyond the school curriculum. Take me for example, do you remember that eighth grader who developed an interest in psychology? I taught myself about psychology through the internet by reading articles, watching videos related to psychology, and watching movies (where I would take time to analyze actors' behaviours in their settings.) I also learned about psychology through books, my first psychology book being given to me by my dad, and then many more given to me by my girlfriend. Then I made sure that my education path aligned with my passion: classes such as psychology in eleventh grade, and research papers in my English classes about my social working program in college. My friend Jesse suggests that school should be a learning environment that is based on experience and promotes failure; a safe environment where you should be able to learn from your mistakes and have someone beside you who can give you constructive feedback.

On March 8, 2022, there was a slight change to the school curriculum due to the use of technology, especially for the hard sciences in grades one to eight taken effect on the 2022-2023 school year. This new curriculum will focus on an update of the STEM program, where first sixth-grade students will learn about the basics of coding so that in sixth grade, they could code flying machines. Children in ninth grade are also going to learn about emerging technology such as AI, the importance of locally grown foods, the impact of food on your physical and mental health, and analyze social, economic, and environmental impacts such as climate change[40]. This is great since it shows that the minister of education is trying to change the science and math program, however, there are other programs that should be offered in schools, such as a class educating students about Capitalism, the study of oneself, and standardization on sexual education throughout Canada.

Let me tell you something, life is unpredictable. For teachers to be able to change the education system and the curriculum, there are a couple of questions we would have to ask ourselves. First of all, the class being taught should give students the tools to solve problems going on in their personal life before fixing problems in the world. If you cannot create a healthy world within you, then you won't create a healthy world outside, since your imagination is a preview of life's

---

[40] *Ontario unveils new science curriculum focused on engineering design, coding | CBC News*. CBC. March 8th, 2022,

upcoming attractions. If all you are thinking about is negativity, then you won't be able to detach yourself from the fact that the world has a bunch of problems *"The world has ninety-nine problems, and your mindset is one"*.

The second element is finding effective solutions, and as I have talked about it starts with you. If you see that the world is full of problems and you are done with complaining about it, you could start looking for more effective solutions[41]. Trying to approach your problem with a more pragmatic solution might let you see something new, and it might lead you to something that could help you.

The third element is that no matter how smart you are, or how much you want to solve a problem, you cannot solve it if you have no resources like money or people that could help. It might be sad to say, but sometimes even if there is a problem, we can't solve it due to a lack of resources. So, in order to see the most of your skills you need to focus on problems where you have easy access to resources so you can find and build solutions. The final element is something that I have already said: if you do a job you enjoy, and that your skills into it, you will get recognized for your effort and prosper from it. The three aspects of an ideal career: Explore, Invest and Deploy. We can explore the world of jobs, and all about how to develop your interests as we continue into what it means to find something that interests you in the next

---

[41] Summary: What makes for a high-impact career? 80,000 Hours. April 10th, 2022,

Problem: *Can't find your interest*, with Jay Shetty's video about finding our interest.

Problem 4

Can't Find Your Passion

Simply put, the tight schedule from all the classes, not having any time to relax, and the lack of knowledge for time management results in this. If you are passionate about a subject learned at school, and you pursue it, then that's excellent, but once you're in school there's little time for you to develop any side hobbies since all your time and energy is spent on your schoolwork.

In elementary school, you are taught a lot of essential skills like how to read, write, count, make friends, and all that good stuff. Some say that we do not need elementary school because you can learn all of those things at home since your parents could teach you. However, you can argue and say that if your parents both work and do not have time for teaching you, then elementary school is best. It is interesting because the way you learn all of those basic things is in a fun, interactive way, and it is based on trial and error. Since it is fun, and you are so young, it's interesting when you take what you learned and spot it in the outside world. For example, you come home after learning how to count to ten, and you end up counting your fingers or counting how many people are in your family to know how many plates are needed for dinner. The same happens when you come home after a science class, and now you feel excited since you can perform that experiment at home. I am well aware that we cannot stay at that stage; however, don't we go to school to learn things that are relevant to what we will be living?

As you move up into the academic years and get older, they just throw things at you and say, "you'll need it for next year" or "you'll see it on the test." Consequently, you just end up learning a bunch of things without knowing where to really apply them unless it is an exam. What happens is that you just learn a bunch of things, you do not really see it outside of school, and you don't realize how important or insignificant it can be. Because you cannot apply it elsewhere than on a test, and it's not relevant to what you want to be, you begin to lose interest. But even in high school, there are times when you can do the same thing in eighth grade, I did a big project on slavery because I'm Black and I rarely learn about those things, it was a wonderful opportunity. Also, in eleventh and twelfth grade, I was able to research social work for English class, and then I looked into what classes I needed to take in college and university, and the job possibilities in the future. But do not get it twisted since this is a prime example of how school should help you pursue your career if you have an idea of what you want to be, they should encourage you to research about it and present it to the class.

A class perfect for helping you find your interests would be an overhaul of the Civics and Career Choices class that is taken by students in tenth grade. Here is how I think it should be divided: Civics class should implement the concept of basic accounting, and money management. This would give students a head starts on the job market, and it could also function as a means for students to make a small amount of money and work to complete their community service hours which is mandatory in the Ontario school system. When it comes to the Career Choices class, you should have the opportunity to pick a place to do an internship so you could get real-life experience of what life on the job looks like. You could pick the job you want, and not only would it allow you to get work experience in your field of interest, but it would also allow for the implementation of necessary life skills. Civics, or even history class, could also use part of its course to break down the fundamentals of the Canadian government's structure, to understand how the country works, which would allow students (especially immigrants) to understand what it means to be a Canadian citizen.

Speaking about that, Artificial Intelligence is something that is going to be part of the future, but high school doesn't talk about the impact it will have on certain jobs. Instead, teachers want to drill in our heads that it is our diplomas and our grades that will open doors to future job opportunities. But if the industry in which you want to work for could save more money by investing in a robot than an employee, then they will do so regardless of their education. This has to do with passion since you do not want to spend all this time studying to then find out that your whole career has been replaced by machinery. As we keep going forward, technology is going to keep advancing, and our society and the job market are going to change with it. We have to do the same in schools so that students can be prepared to deal with the advancements of technology in any field, otherwise, students will be stuck studying for a future that is stuck in the past.

In eleventh grade, I had a social sciences class which combined the subjects of sociology, anthropology, and psychology into a single course. I found myself struggling a lot in the first two modules of this class, and my teacher began to quickly lose patience with me and my struggling grades. He decided to host a parent-teacher meeting with my parents, and I said that I wanted to come here what he had to say. He started by asking y mom if anything is going on at home, which my mom then looked to me to answer. At this point, I realized that there actually is not anything that should be holding me back in this class and that I had to take matters into my own hands. I told all of them that I would do better, and that I would prove it through the results of my upcoming tests. When the psychology module finally came, I educated myself on the subject to improve my understanding. With my efforts and the support of my loving girlfriend, I aced every test that involved the psychology module and showed them that I could do better. This is how I began to grow my passion for psychology, and my interest in the subject is what allowed me to excel in the subject and enjoy studying and working in class.

In general, it is important to pay attention to the lessons. Luckily for me, I never failed a class, but math was the subject that gave me and my family the most trouble. If you end up having a particular interest in a class and you take it, then that can work wonders on your school journey. You will be studying something that interests you and it will be counted as schoolwork at the same time, way to kill two birds with one stone. However, that could backfire if the way it is being taught in school is different from you have learned it before; this could make you see the subject in a different light, and the way its taught might stop you from continuing in the subject later on. Regardless of if it is a gain or loss, you realized that you have less "me time." Also having time for yourself is not bad at all since it is essential for your mental health and it prevents you from reaching a state of burn-out. Do not get me wrong, if you love the class and enjoy the subject, then the grades can be important to you since it's just a self-esteem booster. The other side is that it puts pressure on you to be good at that subject because you like it, and it means something more to you. If you get a bad grade in it, it might hit harder than a bad grade in another class because you have put extra effort into it, and you've still done badly.

In other words, if we know that we are not perfect, then why should perfect grades matter? Take it from the Atlantic, and their video called: *Why Perfect Grades Do Not Matter*.[42] They explain the myth that good grades are the only thing that will get you into a good college or university and that graduating from one of those will guarantee you a high-paying job. Constantly worrying over good grades takes a toll on your self-esteem to the point where you tend to base your worth on the grade you get after a test. On top of that, we know that people who are too focused on their work or getting those "perfect grades" at school do not do well in social settings, since they're too busy chasing those grades which often leads them to be isolated from society.

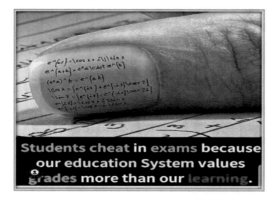

Students cheat in exams because our education System values grades more than our learning.

[42,44] YouTube, The Atlantic, *"why perfect grades don't matter"*, November 30th, 2017,

Do you know why I brought this picture back? Many students turn to cheating to boost their GPAs. A national survey of 24,000 students from seventy high schools in the US found that sixty-four percent of students cheated on their tests. The hardest drug in schools is good grades, and just like real drugs, desperate students turn to dirty tactics to get their high. Now of course you would think that because someone graduated high school with a higher grade, it makes them a happier person or successful in college, but the video made by The Atlantic suggests otherwise.

According to them, a study done in 2014 followed more than 123,000 students into post-secondary education, with an optional admission test. Meaning that if you wanted you could take a test to admit yourself into the University or just let your high school grades do the talking; the goal was to compare the students who submitted a test to those who did not. The researchers found that when it came to participation in college, those with good grades in high school such as SAT or ACT scores did not perform well on the admission test for college but did better in the participation area. And then those with poor grades in high school got better grades on the admission test. *"High school grades demonstrate a pattern of commitment to hard work, but a test taken once in an afternoon only reflects performance on a single given day"* [43] *-The Atlantic*. According to the University of

Michigan, 80% of students base their self-worth on their test scores, so the lower the test score was, the lower their self-esteem plummeted.[44]

Now I understand that if you spend a lot of your time studying and you get a grade that doesn't reflect the amount of time you've spent studying, then that could be disappointing; that's how I felt going through high school math. The problem is the high school grading system has become completely ingrained into students' heads, to the point where many students have lost their creativity and freedom to focus on getting the highest grade. Not only that but because girls succeed more academically than guys on average, this grading system has an even worst effect on girls, in the sense that they push even further to conform to the rules of the school system. Regardless of who you are, when you are in high school every adult around you is trying to shovel the competition for good grades down your throat. They say it will help you get into a good university to find a decent job, but the problem with this is that it motivates you to be good in school for other people, and makes you less interested in doing things for yourself. But if you are the one who's supposed to benefit from good grades and a high-paying job, wouldn't you want to do that on your own time, stress-free? Another thing, the school says it wants to emulate the real world in class, but the thing is in your day-to-day life you do not get graded on your performance.

---

[44] Thomsen, M. *"Get Rid of Grades*. Slate Magazine"*. June 1st 2013,

For example, if you are working at a fast-food place and someone comes in and orders something, you just need to give them what they order, and if they're satisfied and want to, they leave a review. This is the closest thing to getting graded in real life that you will usually come by, but even that doesn't affect you directly as an employee; it affects the reputation of the store, as well as the likelihood of people coming back. But as there is no reward for making an order this has little effect on the employee.

Teachers, would you like to join the conversation about how to not have your students and their parents constantly worry about their grades? According to Elizabeth Gruner,[45] the grading system that we know today was introduced in the 1940s and is used in most schools. When the pandemic started, teachers had to change how they graded their students because of the online shift. Gruner's method broke away from the 'standardized test' system and focused on giving students feedback for their work so they can improve. She would grade them at the end of the semester by having the students submit a portfolio of all of their revised work.

She recommends teachers use this method for three reasons. Number one, she wants her students to focus on the feedback she gave them, instead of the grade. By doing so, her students can reflect on the comments she makes and have a chance to improve. Now I speak for all students when I

---

[45] Gruner, E. *"I no longer grade my students' work – and I wish I had stopped sooner."* The Conversation. March 29th, 2022,

say, if you see a failing grade, you're not paying attention to the comments, since you're worrying about what your parents will think, or you're too frustrated at your failure to process how you could improve. The same thing applies if you see a good grade too; you are excited to show your parents, and you're not going to want to improve in a subject you feel you're good in. For this reason, it is better for students to not receive a grade at all when they are getting feedback, as it will help them focus on improving their work instead of their grades.

For this reason, Gruner thinks it is not fair to grade someone based on how much they could remember since not all students have the same resources to prepare for tests. The second reason that writing feedback on tests does not work is that the content that's being covered has already passed and won't be on the next test. So, what would be smart is to give students back their tests with feedback on all the questions they got wrong and give them the option to redo their tests with related questions. This would allow them to implement their feedback and could help students remember their course content better. The third reason is selfishness: there are even teachers who pride themselves in making their class as hard as possible so that succeeding is more exclusive than inclusive. Students who are determined to succeed will go beyond what's asked to impress the teacher to get that perfect grade and will be disappointed when it doesn't meet their expectations. The teacher should not be allowed to impose their standard of difficulty on the class, it's just an unfair way for the teacher to use their power over their students.

When Gruner introduced this method to her students, she found it difficult to get them to understand that the grades were not what mattered. The students would keep asking for a grade to come with their work, but as she explains that is not the point of the system. The focus is supposed to be on the comments, and how you get a chance to improve without the grade affecting your work. This links into *Problem 1* since it gives a second chance for students to improve and clear instructions to improve their work. The only difference between Gruner's strategy and the one I described in *Problem 1* is where the feedback is used to help students. She uses the feedback to improve on the same work, while I explain that feedback is more helpful for future tests. But the thing is, for both new and old material, feedback will help students understand what they are doing wrong and fix their mistakes. Another thing, I know there are some teachers who openly say they are willing to boost their student's grades or compensate them if they do extra work, and that is good, but you have to negotiate for that extra boost. If you turn in that extra work and the teacher sees it is worthy of boosting your grade by one or two points, then you should run after your teacher and explain why you deserve more than what they said.

An identity crisis is not fun to experience. I know because I experienced one myself at the age of twelve, and it's a point in your life when you wonder why you're doing what you're doing. According to American Psychologist, G. Stanley Hall and his research called "Stress and Storm"[46], concluded that teenagers are mostly known to rebel against adults because they are trying to find their place in society.

According to James E. Marcia, there are four identity statuses: identity diffusion, identity foreclosure, identity moratorium and identity achievement. This goes far beyond what you are going to be when you grow up, it also has to do with your personality, your gender role, sexual orientation etc. I'm going to explain these four statuses in my own words, but I'll have the reference down below if you want clarification. Identity diffusion is before you have gone through an identity crisis and means you haven't thought of developing yourself. Identity foreclosure is when you have no idea what you want to be, but since your parents have already pre-determined a path for you and you'll naturally follow it because it's the only path you know. The perfect example is the idea of "getting your kids into the family business," where your parents determine what type of job you're going to have based on their desires. An identity moratorium is when you didn't experience a crisis just yet, however, you begin to explore different opportunities. For example, I decided to teach myself some of the basics of psychology by reading books to then take it in 11th grade in high school. The final status is Identity achievement, and

---

[46] Hoque, E. G. *Stanley Hall "Storm and Stress" Theory- B. Ed Notes.* Educere Centre. July 5th, 2022.

that's when you've finished exploring your possibilities and you decide **on your own** what will be the best choice for you. [47]

In conclusion, you're wondering what this has to do with passion. Well for one, if a student has no idea what they want to be, then it's a good thing that they explore their choices since you never know where it will bring you. The problem is that the standardized testing system doesn't help students by allowing them to improve in the subject matter. It forces students to have one chance at a topic and if they don't get it, well that's too bad because another one is up next. Just like a passion you need to have the freedom to develop it for yourself, if someone imposes it onto you, you won't want to try it out. Without being given any room to care about the subjects, your productivity, creativity, and innovation go out the window. A change in the approach to learning could help improve these things; an idea supported by the "happiness advantage," an experiment led by Shawn Achor that I talked about previously.

According to Daniel H. Pink, and his book: _Drive,_[48] there are two types of motivators. Motivation 1.0 was to ensure our survival, focusing on our basic needs such as finding food, water, and mates for reproduction. But as we evolved, our motivators did as well: motivation 2.0. This type of motivation was for seeking rewards and avoiding

[47] _Marcia Four Identity Statuses._ January 1st 2021.
[49,50] Daniel H. Pink | The official site of author Daniel Pink. 2021. _Drive | Daniel H. Pink._ May 27th, 2021.

punishment. Now according to him, this is where jobs come in and it operates on this same type of reward system since the reward is getting paid and the punishment to avoid is getting fired. However, in the 1900s Harry F. Harlow conducted a study on eight rhesus monkeys to solve a mechanical puzzle. Without any instructions, the monkeys had fun trying to solve it, but as soon as he gave them raisins, the monkeys put more effort into solving the puzzles, and that was a third motivator called motivation 3.0, or "Intrinsic motivation." Now the fact that this is a book about school, some of you could argue:

"Oh, it's the same for students, if we give them a test and tell them it's formative, they won't give it their all; but as soon as we introduce the grades and give them a summative test, they apply themselves."

And do you know what? I used to think you're right, and I think I'm talking on behalf of every student when I say it's something that's commonly believed.

However, this is when the "reward/punishment" system can backfire, as shown in an experiment done on preschoolers. The preschoolers of Group A were told that they would get a reward after drawing, while the preschoolers of Group B were told they would get the reward before they started drawing and the preschoolers of Group C didn't get any and were simply told to draw freely. After the experiment, Pink concluded that the kids from groups B and C enjoyed drawing more in class and after the experiment, whereas group A stopped drawing and didn't like it after the experiment was over. *"Offering rewards or punishments in the wrong circumstances can also diminish work performance. Being promised a reward often means that people will work up to the point the reward is given, and then stop working. In some cases, rewards can push out good behaviour by encouraging cheating and unethical behaviour. On top of that, reward-oriented thinking means focusing on short-term benefits, rather than thinking in the long term[49]"*-Daniel H. Pink.

When the Joe Rogan Experience had Dr. Phil as a guest, they talked about how not everyone is the same, the video is called: *Everyone Is Not Equal*.[50] They talked about how everyone needs to find their own path, and not feel bad if they aren't good at a certain subject; because unless we're talking about the simple biology of being human, everyone isn't equal. However, if we focus on this book for a moment, schools are supposed to help us find what we want in life. Honestly, it comes from a good place but grading everyone on everything regardless of their abilities puts some people in front of others. Consequently, those who are behind feel left out and are compared to the ones who are ahead, making them feel worse. Even Joe Rogan said, *"Once you do something you're good at, you can accept not being good at*

[51,52] YouTube, JRE clips "Everyone Is Not Equal" February 26th, 2019,

other things. It's much easier to find the thing that you're good at regardless it's gymnastics swimming or painting, or whatever. If you can find a thing that you're good at, it will give you a feeling of self-worth, and you won't need to be good at everything. And you can enjoy other people being good at things as well"[51]

My perfect example is when I was in high school. I would always compare myself to my girlfriend's ability to understand math and sciences, the things that she's good at. I would compare myself to her because I felt external pressure from my parents to be good at math. I felt this pressure because neither I nor they could understand why I didn't get good grades in those subjects, even when I studied like her. That made me feel insecure about my abilities, and I felt ashamed of telling her or my parents about my grades in those classes. That feeling stuck with me until I found my calling in social work, which allowed me to move away from math, now I couldn't care less about math or science and if anything, my love for her grew stronger. This allowed us to grow as a couple because we could be happy in our respective fields and also for each other without the need for competition. What I realized was that the only person we can truly compare ourselves to is our past selves, since that is where we can measure our growth.

There are two areas in finding a passion or something you enjoy. The first aspect is thinking and reflection; the second is action and experimentation. The problem is that he feels like people are doing too much of one category without the other. To balance this out he suggests using reflection to break down and class the things you can do into 4 categories.

- You have expertise in it, but no interest in it.
- You have an interest in it but have no expertise in it.
- You have no expertise in it and no interest in it.
- You have expertise in it, and you have an interest in it. [52]

He wants people to think more thoroughly about what interests them, which is why he wants you to ask yourself a simple question *"What do I enjoy doing?"* He also says you should reflect on the best decision you think you've made in your life because chances are that you knew it was the best decision when you made it, and not because of the result it gave you. If you think about the thought process that gave you that idea, you'll be able to apply that same thought process to future ideas. The second half: action and experimentation. For this part he suggests using all your weekends for a month to do something new, like attending a

---

[52] YouTube, Jay Shetty, "The ONLY VIDEO You Need To Find Your TRUE PURPOSE In Life", January 13th, 2021,

workshop, listening to a podcast (mine for example on Spotify, Apple Podcast, and Google podcast: Just Inwords), or practicing a new skill by yourself, just taking one weekend to try it out. There are eight full days for all four weekends in a month, which gives you at least eight new things to try out and reflect on.

To conclude he says that if you put thinking and reflection together with action and experimentation, in one of the things you did in that month you'll find something that stands out. He says that if you take your time and if you work on that one thing from there, it has the potential to become a passion. I understand how this could seem very generalized, but here's a way to apply it to your class choices. The first part can be applied by thinking of the various subjects you can take and trying out the class that introduces it. Then as you go through your classes you see if any of them fall into any of these categories:

- You don't feel like you are learning anything, and you aren't good in class. (**You have no interest and no expertise**)
- You don't feel like you are learning anything, but you have good grades in the class. (**You have no interest, but you have expertise**)
- You want to learn more about the subject, but you don't do well in tests. (**You have interest, but have no expertise**)

- You want to learn more about the subject, and you do well in tests as well. (**You have interest, and you have expertise**)

Then when you have a bit more choices in your class selection, you could decide to further explore the classes you've been introduced to, because if it was only the tip of the iceberg and it interested you, don't you want to find out what lies beneath? Now for the action and experimenting, regardless of if it's in high school or post-secondary, you usually have a chance to evaluate a class for a couple of weeks and drop it early, without it penalizing your school year. I understand that you can't jump from class to class to see what works for everything since other students are taking classes as well, but that's where thinking and reflecting come into play so that you can look into what speaks to you beforehand and make the best choices for your classes from there. The good news is, as you progress through high school, the more freedom you are given to choose classes that are more personalized to you. For example, math and science are offered as crash courses in ninth and tenth grade but in eleventh and twelfth you could choose which math or which science you want to follow.

Given the fact that other students do it as well and it could get complicated, that's why you have to make sure you're changing classes because you don't like it as opposed to the workload being too hard thinking going into another class would make the load easier. And for two, in life you change and so could your interest and going from hobby to hobby only gives you more general skills eventually. However, we still need to acknowledge the minor difference between someone changing hobbies because it doesn't suit them anymore as opposed to it being too hard and switching to something else just looks easier.

Things you can control:

Your beliefs
Your attitude
Your thoughts
Your perspective
How honest you are
Who your friends are
What books you read
How often you exercise
The type of food you eat
How many risks you take
How kind you are to others
How you interpret situations
How kind you are to yourself
How often you say "I Love You"
How often you say "Thank you"
How you express your feelings
Whether or not you ask for help
How often you pratice gratitude
How many times you smile today
The amount of effort you put forth
How you spend and invest your money
How much time you spend worrying
How often you think about the past
Whether or not you judge other people
Whether or not you try again after the setback
How much you appreciate the things you have

Problem 5

We All Learn Differently

In 1983, psychologist Howard Gardner proposed that there are nine forms of intelligence that affect the way and speed that different people learn, and they are broken down into the different forms of thought that people use in each of these respective fields:

- **Verbal-linguistic intelligence-** The ability to communicate effectively with others.
- **Mathematical-logical intelligence-** The ability to understand logical concepts and mathematics.

- **Musical intelligence-** The ability to play musical instruments and understand musical theory.
- **Visual-Spatial intelligence-** The ability to visualize abstract and real concepts.
- **Kinesthetic intelligence-** The ability to understand one's own body and physical ability.
- **Interpersonal intelligence-** The ability to talk to and understand other people.
- **Intrapersonal intelligence-** The ability to understand oneself.
- **Naturaliste intelligence-** The ability to understand the natural world.
- **And Existential intelligence-** The ability to see the greater picture of something in greater depth.[53]

Along with those intelligences you also have the diverse ways that each student learns best. From being a dominantly visual person, an auditive person or a kinesthetic type of learner. With all that, there are some subjects that you will have an easier time understanding than others. There might be a subject that you understand but the way it's delivered it's not your cup of tea or you can't understand regardless of the efforts you put in. What I'm saying is it's

[53] Marenus, M. Simplypsychology.org. June 9th 2020,

never your fault if you don't understand something unless you're trying to not understand by not participating.

The problem here is that the school doesn't realize that each student has a predominant form of intelligence, so measuring it based upon one form of results will leave some students feeling "behind," since they aren't having their form of intelligence nurtured. You just need to right tools to advance, the problem is what teachers call the right tools is extra homework, or a meeting with your parents to try and understand what's going on (which always ends up being that you aren't trying hard enough). What could work to fix this is the idea of the teacher taking time to help students who aren't going with the flow of the class. This means that the student isn't able to learn this concept as easily because their predominant intelligence isn't in tune with the subject, so they will need to be taught in a different way for the subject to be adapted to them.

Take me for example, when I had a parent-teacher meeting to talk about my grades, the whole conversation was focused on how to get me to improve in class. There is never any discussion about how to make the class more adaptable to the student's type of intelligence, which a mistake because it blames the student for failing even when they are putting in the effort. Taking my ninth-grade math teacher as an example, he decided to conduct the meeting by taking work from the math book and comparing it to my papers; he showed how both of these didn't add up and said there was a problem because I didn't understand. And you're right there's a problem but it wasn't the book, nor the teacher, nor me; the problem was that the teaching method wasn't right for me to understand the subject, and I simply didn't know what I was doing. I continued to apply myself however, which helped a bit in the next year as my tenth-grade math teacher was more helpful at explaining and answering questions. However, this would begin to return to the same problem once the actual tests rolled around, and I once again began to struggle in class.

If you ask questions and still put effort into what you're doing, most of the time you should still be able to understand enough to get through the class and pass the tests. It might just be me and my teachers, but I remember most of them would say on tests, *"Even if you don't get the right answers, you will get points if you can show your thought process and it makes sense."* regarding developmental questions. This is especially important for classes like math or science, where oftentimes the questions can be too hard to get the exact right answer for most students. For these questions, it's still worth giving it a shot by trying your best to find your way to the right answer, because even if you don't get everything correctly, the closer you were to the right way to solve the questions, the higher our mark will be, even if the definitive answer isn't exactly correct. My question for teachers is this: if you allow students to answer questions through different paths of logic, why can't you also give students different paths for learning as well? If we answer the questions differently, clearly, we learned the concept differently as well.

Let me give an example, I have an IEP, and it says that on certain exams I am entitled to answer certain questions verbally. When those questions would come up, I would write down keywords beside them and then would leave class with my teacher so that I could answer him verbally on the spot. My point here is that without that IEP, I wouldn't have had the tools at my disposal to effectively answer the questions, which would have caused me to get a lower grade than I deserved. But it shouldn't be because of an IEP that they should consider another method, every student should have an **I**ndividual **E**ducation **P**lan to help them obtain their best method of learning in school.

Let's suppose that school is a hospital, with every classroom being a hospital room designed for a specific procedure with a doctor who's an expert in that field. It's fair enough to think that the patients who are in the room for an eye exam, need an eye exam that holds up to modern standards. Here's the thing, the doctor who gives you the eye exam will only be able to examine you by referring himself to what he's learned during his training. But with time, the procedures that are done for the eye exam have changed, but the doctor hasn't received new training. Since the time that your teacher was a student in teacher's college, the way people view learning has evolved: they didn't learn about the different forms of intelligence or the different ways to approach teaching so students can better understand.

This role is then passed on to the teacher who has a class to teach, students who need help, and a strict period to complete the curriculum. Teachers should apply the concept of the nine forms of intelligence when instructing their students so that they can optimize students learning. I do not need to tell you that all the students in the class have distinct levels of knowledge and ability for each subject, and you'll find that it's linked to their predominant form of intelligence. This is why teachers should stop trying to shove homework down students' throats, and instead focus on nurturing students' abilities through their best way of learning.

As you've realized by now, I'm not particularly good at math. I was reminded of this for the first three years of my high school, as general maths is mandatory from ninth to eleventh grade in the Ontario school system. One thing I noted going through my math classes is how my learning was affected by my chemistry with the math teacher. My ninth-grade math teacher was a great guy. He was always welcoming, he loved to play soccer with other students, and he greeted everyone with respect; I was always happy to see him outside of class. But despite his great personality, his teaching method wasn't good for me to properly understand the subject. His style of teaching was only good for people who already had mathematical intelligence, which could be summed up in his work motion "do it quick but do it well" given the fact that we had nine modules to go through. He would be harsh on people who weren't good in math and tried his best to fit every student into the same mould. This brute force method of teaching led lots of students who were bad at math, like me, to fall through the cracks.

After that year was finished, the only thing I remember thinking was "I don't want to be in his class next year," and luckily for me, I wasn't. In my tenth-grade math class, I enjoyed my class a little more since I was relieved that I didn't have my teacher from last year but that didn't stop my grades from slipping. Therefore, to not go through what I did last year, my parents decided to pair me up with a tutor. When it comes to my tenth-grade teacher, she was more comprehensive of people's level of understanding and was more patient when it came to those who had more questions. Our class atmosphere was very relaxed probably since we only had three modules this year, and she explained things in a more digestible manner since she wasn't good at math herself. At the end of the year, I was able to get sixty-six percent on my final exam and pass the class, which was a huge deal to me, since my confidence in math had been destroyed during the year prior.

And finally, eleventh grade came along. I didn't have a preference for teachers for this year as long as it wasn't the one from ninth grade, which to my relief, it was not. This teacher's style of teaching gave me a balance of both worlds, as a bit felt like gibberish and a bit of it was something with which I could work. For example, right off the bat, he was more open to helping the girls than the guys therefore when I went to ask for help or clarifications I was often met with "Did you look at your notes?" Also, we'd have a fair amount of time to work in groups on certain exercises or he'd give us the entire class to do so luckily for me, my girlfriend and I were in the same class, and we'd often work together, and her help was another factor of my perseverance in the class. I don't remember the number of modules we covered throughout the semester, but the class included a project on finances. The tutoring I received also helped me here, which was one of the reasons why my finance project was a success. In the end, I was able to navigate my way through 11th grade but just like ninth grade I failed the exam but passed the class.

My conclusion is that even if I was the same hardworking student the result of my efforts didn't always pay off due to the class environment. Since as much as it is your job as a student to make sure you're able to do the work that's assigned to you, it's also your job as a teacher to establish the environment so that the student could feel comfortable to try and reach their full potential to feel fulfilled. For example, as I mentioned already, I was always eager to answer questions and actively participate but not every teacher was open and patient if I'd get the answer wrong, and unlike my ninth-grade teacher, the others will invite me to think about the answer I gave then now that I know the answer. Once I found out I had dyscalculia, I tried my best to put all the luck on my side until me knowing it was not mandatory in twelfth grade, I didn't take it. We are all different people, who think in diverse ways. No one should feel ashamed for how fast or slow they learn in comparison to others; the important thing is that we are able to learn no matter what. And I know in the heat of the moment it's not easy to not feel ashamed of yourself when you struggle to understand something, especially when your parents and your teachers are all putting pressure on you to pass. I remember when I failed one of my tests in tenth-grade math, I let out a burst of anger in frustration, which is reform me, so it surprised some people. Because of this one of my friends came to talk to me and give me a pep talk, which was something that I needed at the time. I remember how difficult it was for me to explain to him my struggle because he was doing fine in the class himself. Even when I was talking to my friend, I realized that the difference in our grades caused a gap in communication between us, because someone with higher grades couldn't understand someone with lower grades than them. They can't understand the frustration of failing repeatedly when you put effort into a test, or how grades separate students into a weird 'grade-cast' system. It's difficult to move away from these things, even when looking back at it, the grades themselves are not as important as they felt back then. In the end, it's like my dad use to say, *"La vie n'est pas une course, c'est un marathon."* Instead, teachers in the schools should use the grades obtained by the students in the tests to auto-evaluate themselves, and unlike the other schools who publish their global grades to show everyone who has the better school, they keep it to better themselves. Without grades being stuck into the minds of students, they are freed from having to compare themselves to others, and from having to hold up to their parents' expectations. They are given the opportunity to go through school without being sorted into an academic caste system which judges people based on the grades on a paper.

As I said earlier, the level of difficulty of any semester in school depends on the number of classes you have because each of their workloads gets harder to manage in the timeframe you are given. When a semester is packed with too many of these hard classes this often forces students to rush their studying just so they can pass their tests. However, it leads to them also forgetting most of what they learned after their semester is over. Therefore, when you begin a class in a new year, you're bound to have holes in your memory for the things you've forgotten. On top of that, especially when you go on summer break, you leave those things behind for months on end since there is still a time when no student is touching a book and no teacher is correcting an exam and both are just appreciating the break.

Take me for example, my ninth-grade math class was in the first semester of school, and it just so happened that my tenth-grade math class would take place in the second semester of the next year. This meant that I wouldn't touch a math book for over a year before my next math class, because math is a bad subject for me, even relearning something is a bigger struggle. And because the class is supposed to keep adding onto last year's subject, the teacher only takes about a week to recover every that was passed through last year, and as a result, it's almost easier to do one step forward and two steps back. It's like that with everything, if you don't practice something for a long time, you're bound to get rusty at it and forget how to do it properly. But then teachers respond with **"Well it's your fault that you didn't study over the holidays"** … yes, because of course, what you're supposed to do during a *break* is work? And if you think about it, it's not the teacher's fault. The curriculum forces teachers to be rushed with their work, instead of fully bringing their students up to speed so that they can understand everything moving forward. The good thing about online learning though is that it lets teachers communicate with their students early. What they should do is give them a preparation package, with information and practice for them to get up to speed before the start of the semester, so that the transition is less rough for students who haven't practiced the subject in a while.

Have you ever used a GPS? Think of the GPS as your teacher and it's teaching you how to go somewhere. On the other hand, there are multiple ways to get there, and you're allowed to choose your route; the GPS is simply there to give you the best direction possible. However, if for some reason you take a wrong turn, it doesn't tell you "You're a failure, turn back and go home. You'll never succeed." It adjusts to where you are and tells you how to get to your destination from there. The way the tests are made is based on 'what you were taught,' and your grade is supposed to represent 'what you understand.' Your grade is based on how much you remember, and they assume that you can memorize more than half of the content will determine whether you pass or not. I know that some teachers say, "We give the same test to every student so that everyone gets the same chance." Well, I'm sorry to break your bubble, but that's not going to happen because each student is built differently. From where they come from, to what type of intelligence they have, to what method of learning works for them, and then the fact that every test is based on memorization, and the fact that everyone's brain doesn't work well for the test format. Take me for example, apart from my exam for my psychology class, when we had a test on anything, I wouldn't do well; even though I would understand the concepts of the class and keep up with my peers.

Speaking about conversation, teamwork is a crucial factor in education since it's something that was going to have to do in our everyday lives. Therefore, most classes should be equally divided into half lecturing and half teamwork and discussion about what has been learned. Some people, me included, learn better through discussion, and taking that away from us isn't optimal. These students spend most of the time participating in class and typically try to show their understanding through class participation. The problem is many of these students struggle when it comes to writing tests, which is why it's unfair for them to only be graded through only a single means which doesn't fit well for their understanding. There are also the people who struggle with being able to socially communicate their ideas, and who instead excel at demonstrating their understanding through tests. These people should still have the option of showing their work through paper, but it shouldn't be the only form of testing available to grade a student's understanding. Everyone has separate ways of being able to show their understanding of a concept and judging them in a single way that we deem fit will box them into a suboptimal way of communicating their understanding of a subject. Let's take Socrates for an example: if you brought him back to life right now and told him to write an essay in a three-paragraph format about his philosophy, he would not convey his message as eloquently as he could. It would lower his idea because the format doesn't work for him, and this isn't different for a student and how he is graded, it's unfair and it's damaging the potential of students learning everywhere.

Albert Einstein once said,

"Everyone is smart, but if you judge a fish by its ability to climb a tree, it will live its whole life thinking it's stupid."

54

---

[54] "Albert Einstein Quotes About Intelligence | A-Z Quotes". *A-Z Quotes*, 2021,

Problem 6

Lecturing

L ooking back on the previous problems I have discussed throughout this book, nothing can really define the lecture format better than the idea of **"Outdated Learning**." *"A one size fits all approach is not the way to go about education"* [55]- Sal Khan, founder of Khan Academy.

Nowadays, you have all the information on the internet at your fingertips, and anyone can learn anything they want. The only problem is that this can be a double-edged sword, as anything can be put on the internet without proper regulation or fact-checking. On one end, before the internet was developed, knowledge and information were only found

---

[55] *Top 10 Sal Khan Quotes*. Brainy Quote. July 16th, 2022,

in library books, or you would have to attend a post-secondary education if you wanted to learn any profession more thoroughly. But post-secondary educations come with a heavy financial cost, and the teachers know that your future depends on them but have no incentive to put effort into teaching because they know there is no competition for their position. The good thing about the internet is that it can allow you to become your teacher since you have all the theory right at your fingertips. And since it's on the internet, there's the added benefit of competition between the people trying to teach you, so you can have access to a competent teacher who knows what he's talking about. Also, you can learn on your own time without the pressure of exams, deadlines, or a teacher telling you how something should be done; but best of all, on the internet, most of these things are also free. The only downside of having things on the internet is that the information found in colleges and universities is highly classified, and it can be confusing to figure out on your own what's real and what's not. So, the advantage of having a teacher who studies in that field is that you can trust that they know what they're talking about, and that what they are teaching you is the right thing.

Lecturing it's forcefully changing someone's opinion about something from a position of superiority without any interaction. Learning from a professional in that field would be more interesting, since you're learning from someone who's already worked in the field firsthand, instead of learning from someone who only knows the theory. The problem is that lectures are also a flawed medium for teaching these concepts to people. This format forces people to do nothing but listen and blindly accept what they hear. They cannot ask questions to further develop their understanding of a topic, even if what they are being taught might not be factual but just the teacher's opinion. Think of a sex ed class, if the teacher/school has homophobic beliefs, it's going to teach their student's to be homophobic. The problem here is that students have no room to question this, even if many might disagree with what's being taught.

The classes are also big, which forces everyone into a scenario where they have to fend for themselves, with less opportunity to connect with their peers. The worst thing though relates to what I said in the previous Problem: the lecture format makes test grades the most important thing to measure someone's understanding because the class is usually too big for a professor to assess any individual personally. These problems represent why the lecture format becomes the least effective format of learning for students because it forces the student to do all the work.

My digestion class is a class where you get help digesting what you've eaten, sounds cool right? Every teacher should encourage students to manage their time accordingly and focus on the digestion of content that the students have to go through for both their class and others. The National Health Organization defines Bulimia as *"Bulimia nervosa is a serious, potentially life-threatening eating disorder characterized by a cycle of bingeing and compensatory behaviours such as self-induced vomiting designed to undo or compensate for the effects of binge eating.* "[56] If you think about it, that's essentially what school forces every student to do: binge their learning until their minds are full of undigested content and then regurgitate it for an exam. No wonder it feels good to be able to forget about a test once you've written it because you've been released from holding in all that content that's been doing nothing but clogging your head and stressing you out.

Just like food, knowledge needs enough time to digest so that it can be integrated and used. Therefore, if you eat too much, your mind won't be able to process it all and you'll just end up vomiting most of it out. And just like when you eat a big meal before going to bed, if you study too hard at

[56]"Bulimia Nervosa". *National Eating Disorders Association,* June 9th, 2021,

night you won't be able to fall asleep because your energy will be concentrated on digesting. Believe me, I've done it before, and it has only resulted in me sleeping in through my afternoon classes. Think about it, if you eat a big meal before bed, you won 't be able to sleep properly because your body's active, digesting everything you've consumed before you can rest. Well, it's the same thing for studying for a test: if you cram your test material the day before and then sleep on it, chances are you will spend the rest of your night thinking about the content instead of getting sleep, which is bound to damage your performance the next day. If you think about how most people eat, it's usually broken down into three big meals in a day, with snacks if you get hungry in between. So, the question is, why do we treat studying so differently when we need to digest things the same way? It would naturally be best to break studying down into chunks, simple portions that can easily be digested like meals and snacks throughout the day. If this sounds familiar, it's the logic used by the Pomodoro technique, which also explains that your study periods should be in descending sizes throughout the day, meaning your largest study period is in the morning and they should get smaller throughout the day, so you aren't stuck digesting something too heavy at night.

My friend Pierce once told me, *"Don't let the fear of failure bring you to fail,"* so if you have a test that's really heavy on your mind, don't try to ignore it to get it out of your head. If you do, you will find yourself having less time to study, and that will put you in a position of having to digest too much content in too little time. If you fear that you don't have enough time, then try the time management technique I've been using since eighth grade and use an agenda to break things down into digestible chunks. This would allow you to also see where your portions of free time throughout your week are, and it could allow you to optimize your time to make the best progress in whatever you need to learn. For example, during the early days of high school, I would usually focus on getting things done at the beginning of the week, because the later half would be packed with other things I had to get done.

When you eat, the saliva and your teeth work together to break down the food to prepare it for digestion, then it goes into your body and gets digested. From there, the nutrients that are essential for your body go to their respective places, and the rest comes out as natural waist. This means that biologically you only retain what you need, and it's similar to what you learn. You could fill your plate with food all you want, but what you think is good, and what your body thinks is good (and wants to keep), can be completely different. In other words, food for your body, s like knowledge for your brain (and that's why it's called food for thought). But just like with food, there's a limit to how much will be retained as you consume, and in the case of knowledge that means that most of what you learn in the short term will not be remembered eventually. In general, you'll remember the essentials of whatever concept you learn, but what the school curriculum considers things you "need to know," and what you attain, are not only completely different but are also not reflected in standardized tests. This is also why we tend to do better in optional classes, instead of the courses that are considered essential; since the classes are less dense, their information is more interesting, which means we remember it more easily. Whether it's learning or eating, at the bottom line it's all just a question of your body's ability for processing. And just like healthy eating can help you stay physically healthy, healthy learning can help keep you mentally fit.

To conclude, lecturing someone about anything is just boring, it doesn't bring anyone into a position of active learning, and seeing that that's the goal of a lecture, it's just a bad medium for teaching. Instead, a classroom environment should be focused on discussing the topic in question with the class and try to vary the learning atmosphere since new environments will trigger distinct parts of the brain and improve learning. Let's say you're a physical education or biology teacher, during the fall and the spring you should bring students outside if possible because it's a more exciting environment and it gets students more engaged with the class. These classes can also be made more interactive to get students more involved in their subjects: bringing your gym class to school sports competitions, having math competitions to promote teamwork, and highlighting the artistic expression of English classes are simple ways to improve students' interest without having to spend lots of money. Tom Hierck, educator, and author of multiple books explains the big problem with the education system: It's far behind by saying; *"21st century kids are being taught by 20th century adults using 19th century curriculum and techniques on an 18th century calendar!"*[57]

[57] Hierck, T. Best TOM HIERCK Quotes - The Cite Site. June 5th, 2022.

Problem 7

The Inevitable. The Unexpected.

The Pandemic.

The reality is, pretty much no one was ready for a global pandemic to happen out of the blue. So, when COVID-19 did arrive in Canada, most facilities were left scrambling, most of them having to shut down or find a way to move online. In fact, the only person who seemed to have predicted this was the premier of Ontario who cut school funding for the province before it was even necessary. Before the pandemic and they shut down schools for good, teachers were on strike, so sometimes we'd have a four-day week once a month, then it went twice a month for two days a week until March 12, 2020. Because the pandemic made schools shut down, that's when I unofficially graduated: I marched out of school (pun intended) without exams, prom, or formal graduation. How ironic is that? Back in *Problem 4,* I talked about how much time teachers from different countries spent preparing for their classes versus actually teaching students. Well during the teacher's strike, my teachers were only showing up at the same time as most students and didn't have the time to prepare. The thing is, regardless of these strikes, teachers were forced to move to the online way of learning when COVID-19 hit. Everyone had to scramble to make it work out, and it demonstrated how quickly some teachers were to adapt to a new system. Many teachers fell behind however, being unable to work properly under the new online conditions, which is why the province decided that grades would not drop any lower than the first term for the rest of the winter semester.

To sum up my college experience online, it wasn't the best, but it wasn't the worst. To start, they focused on our comprehension, and when they saw that college had to be online, the program coordinator remodelled the whole curriculum to adapt to our new conditions. The professors also taught things very differently compared to high school; they were against the idea of having to memorize most things and made the class content accessible at all times for students. The teachers focused more on the comprehension of the content instead of its memorization, which showed me how much better learning can be when teachers used different methods of learning. I also appreciated that they encouraged critical thinking, and welcomed different ideas which were lots of fun, and entertaining discussions. Most of my classes were divided into two parts: one half was focused on listening to the course content, and the other half was set up to group students in teams and discuss the content of the lecture. While I was in college, I met some people who had children with them while they were in online lectures, and they often wouldn't be able to sit down with everyone while the teacher gave the lesson. To make the lessons more accessible for people in situations like this, the teachers would record their lectures and put them up on the school's learning platform to allow people to access the content whenever they wanted. Not only did that allow students to listen to the recording anytime they want, but it also allowed them to take the time to properly understand what was being said since they have control of the speed of the lecture.

In college, we were also given a learning platform that allowed us to download all the content of our classes, which was especially convenient for our exams which were open books as long as you cited your sources. The college quickly understood that on the internet, it's impossible to control what you can look up, so as a compromise they made all the tests open book as long as you cited them properly. Also, you need to have some knowledge of the subject to look for it in the book, right?

Let's suppose that you're going shopping: I know that I couldn't go without my wallet, my mask (for COVID-19), and of course my shopping list. If I don't bring my list with me, or if I don't know what I'm looking for, I will either forget what to buy or end up buying the wrong thing. The same thing applies to a test, if I don't come prepared with a little memory card, and take the time to understand its contents, I'm going to end up failing my test. Some people say that open-book tests waste the time of the student, and there are other people who say that it's helpful if you know what you're doing. The good news is, access to class content in an open-book exam is completely optional, so if you worry that it'll waste your time, you can choose to do it as if it were a closed-book test instead. I personally think that open-book tests should be allowed for two reasons:

Number one, it reduces the amount of people who fail because they can't memorize definitions or formulas. Therefore, having that book beside you can refresh your memory and remove the hesitation of putting down an answer. I understand that looking for it in a book can waste time, but not knowing what to put where, or having to take the time to remember would also waste time. I really think teachers should encourage open-book tests, or another option is to make the test partially open-book, by having the students do the test without help from flashcards but give them the opportunity to look through the book after they are done if they need help to remember minor concepts. Think about it, doing that will not only help the students by giving them the time to focus on their test, but it will also stop them from doing mistakes that don't reflect their understanding of the subject.

Number two, it takes away the stress of trying to remember everything, because students know how prepared they are for a test if they understand the content. The problem is if the test is a closed book there is a much higher chance that the student may encounter a definition they understand, but may not be sure of, and that could jeopardize their grade even if they understand what they are doing. Even if you are good at remembering these concepts, there is bound to come a time when you'll wish you had access to the class content simply to get a quick refresher. The problem is, this is also where cheating is born because, in times of need where the student can't remember what he needed, he'll find another way to get the answer even if it isn't honest.

Another good thing about learning online is that it allows you to have total control in managing your time for teaching the class. This is one of the reasons why teaching students in middle school and high school about time management is so important because it's applied in full force once you get to college. For example, one of my college classes had the whole course content online before it was even covered in class, so if you wanted to know what would be discussed in future classes you could go onto the site and do some independent learning. The website also gave told us what content each test would cover, what projects we would be doing, and what pages from the manual we would have to read for each class. This format allows students to go at their own pace, as some students will go beyond their lectures and study ahead of time, and it allows others who are busy doing other things to catch up on their own time. Another aspect that's interesting about online learning is that since no one knew about this and no one was expecting this, we get to experience everyone's life outside of school since that's what we're living. So, what that means is some teachers are willing to allow certain accommodations such as more time on a test or recorded classes on the online platform. Everyone has had to restart from zero, because your teachers have had to reorganize their curriculum for online learning, and students have had to adapt their study methods as well.

One of the negative parts of online learning is the struggle to find proper motivation, which others can see as a lack of discipline. However, as you spend your time working in one place, you will naturally become attuned to your surroundings, *"Location has energy, and time has memory"*- Jay Shetty's book *'Think like a Monk.'* Over time, you will develop a habit that will allow you to improve your discipline over time. Every location you go to has its energy or vibe, and some of these environments are optimal for studying conditions. That's what helped me, I found a location that helped me focus, and I found myself over time improving as it gave me the discipline to study without distractions. When I was in school before covid, I would often use this method. I would go to a place where studying was natural for me, and then when I would leave it and go home, I could feel the energy of discipline go as well. This was the problem that came with online learning, as the optimal learning location isn't necessarily in the household, which means you might have to make space for discipline while also fighting the distractions that might be there as well.

For example, during the pandemic, I would do school in my bedroom. The problem is, I also sleep, write, watch TV, and everything else you normally do in a bedroom. Of course, there are other rooms in the house where I could have studied. However, no matter where it is in the house, there are distractions that stop the flow of work, and that's why you still need to work hard on developing discipline. Another disadvantage is the fact that we do a lot of teamwork, however doing that is tiring because the atmosphere of the school isn't there, so it's harder to focus and it's a lot less fun. The fact that we are all online also means that you can turn off your camera during class, which means it's a lot easier to disengage yourself from the class and get distracted by other things, and teamwork on teams doesn't work (pun intended). And think about it, if you're at school and your cellphone rings, the energy of the room tells you not to answer, and instead ignore the phone call and get back to work. Now consider your office space at home, if you get a phone call while you are on Zoom, it's a lot easier to just turn off the camera and answer the call. This is not only a distraction, but it removes you from the flow of the class, making you a lot less interested in paying attention in the future.

As I talked about earlier in *Problem 4*, the difficulty of a semester is completely dependent on the number and type of classes you're faced with, which is why I was happy to find that college made each term more manageable. Compared to the breakdown of my high school semester, college worked on trimesters, with three different modules and each of them lasted five weeks. The one problem with this system is that my classes graded their students through monthly projects, which was exhausting to do repeatedly. Especially since we are thinking about a project that reflects an ongoing need in a specific community that can't be done in the course of a month. Because college also functions based on trimesters, everything is very rushed too. Things begin slow, but then quickly ramp up into a stressful situation that can get out of control. This is what happened to me, and it caused me to lose motivation and I found out that I needed to really push myself to regain my discipline. The fact that this system caused me, and many of my peers this much stress, tells me something is wrong.

It's not the only college that's been affected by the pandemic, however. Schools in general had to undergo changes to their safety protocols and adapt to online learning methods too. However, the students in high school suffered the worst of the changes to their system. In an attempt to minimize exposition to COVID-19, schools concentrated students into two-month "quadmesters" (which means four terms), where the student would only take two classes per term instead of the regular 4. But this system wasn't all bad; the fact that the students could focus on two classes gave them more class time each day, which helped them fully understand the material they were learning. In a way, this can be a new way to revolutionize school and it's also a way to cope with the integration of computers with modern-day schooling. The pandemic clearly shook things up and caused lots of problems with the system, but in a way that might not be a completely terrible thing. Now that we've had a taste of offline learning, we can use the best parts of it to help us advance the school system by giving students new options. If they want to do their classes online, or maybe take quadmesters instead of semesters, why should it be something we deny them?

When they decided to close the schools for good, even if I was technically done going to school, according to the twelfth-grade curriculum we weren't done. Therefore, the minister of education made the teachers create an online module and have students have at least three hours a day of schooling it could be via video chats, online work, studying or tests. But between you and me, this is when the teachers experienced what the students were talking about when they said that they didn't want to think about school when they got home and spend time with their families. The students could experience what the teachers were going through as parents, spouses or how hard it could be to correct or produce something. Because since everyone was dealing with their home life now attending online schooling became a drag, now add on the fact that you're in your senior year during your last three months, you've had enough. The point here is that even if school was closed, we had to find a way to keep our education flowing. That's when online platforms and part-time in-person schooling comes into play.

Because we're only hoping that this is the first and last time, we have to experience this type of thing. When we become COVID free that we need to go back to our old ways, we could implicate what the high schools were doing during the pandemic and when it comes to college attending an online class can be for those who either live too far, have an early class or both. Because the goal is to revolutionize the way we go to school, and this can work, and it could be easier for those who learn independently because the teacher gives the work online and you do it in your own time. It could work for those who need a bit of one-on-one time since on the day that you go to school in person, you can clarify with the teacher what you didn't understand, or you schedule a meeting with the teacher and either meet up virtually or in person. And finally, it can increase discussions because of the time you were at home if there's something you didn't understand you can ask and since there's not really a class then you can be with the teacher and you can work on it together because of that not everyone is on the same level of comprehension. But in general, this pandemic has proven that we don't need schools as a facility. Of course, for some classes, it makes it easier to be in a class with the appropriate material, but we've done well with online learning. Because as long as we have the information at our fingertips, which we do because of the internet, therefore all we need is education.

School should function as a meeting point, where students can work and discuss their class content in a social manner. The content itself should be made available online so that the students who work independently can have that option, while other students can benefit from teamwork while they are in person. The one problem with this system is that teachers fear they would lose control of their class if the class content was placed online. However, I think it would have the opposite effect, as more advanced students won't become disengaged with the class while students who are slower would be given more opportunities to understand, as well as catch up. This seems to me like the opposite result of *'losing control,'* and it just means the teacher will have to adapt to a newer curriculum style, which focuses on getting all students prepared for the next upcoming test.

Solutions

New Way to Revolutionize School

Even though school has barely evolved over the last 150 years, this pandemic could be the solution. It could provide an outlet for change so schools can incorporate online platforms. The internet has allowed everyone the opportunity to attend school, it doesn't matter where you are, as long as you have an internet connection you can attend a class from anywhere in the world. In Jay Shetty's video called: *Before 2020 ends, watch this*[58] he teaches a history class to kids in the year 2050 about how the year 2020 was, by showing them a recap of that year. What I find interesting is the way that technology has evolved, and it's used to create a virtual reality but it's better. As technology improves in school, the possibility of the

---

[58] YouTube, Jay Shetty, "Before 2020 ends, watch this" December 31st, 2020,

171

education system being moved to virtual reality will have to be discussed. This might not be a terrible thing though; it could allow students to get their education from anywhere around the globe. This could also help improve the teacher's tools when he teaches the class and allow students to continue their schooling online without distractions from their houses. Something I never thought I would be able to say is that I learned more about staying home than being at school.

The online format of teaching improved the accessibility of content for me, which made studying easier. In-person, we don't have all the notes at our fingertips, and each student is forced to learn with the flow of the class. The online format simply removes these problems and gives the students more autonomy.

The question throughout this whole book was what the use of school is. I think there needs to be a clearer understanding of the purpose of school. School should not be treated as a place where you simply go to learn, it's a place where the students can be social as well. Understanding how to socialize is one of the most principal functions of school, as it prepares us for who we're going to be when we enter the adult world. Because as the new curriculum mentioned in *Problem 3,* the three things we should implement were learning how money works, knowing yourself and how your school life affects your personal life and how to foster good relationships.

In a way school is your like childhood household: your teachers in school play a similar role to your parents,' which is to provide a safe learning environment for you to develop in without consequences, and at the same time guide you down the right path. Think of a baby learning to walk for the first time, even if outside the home there's always something in the way, in the household you clear some space for the child to be able to explore their surroundings safely. The same tactic is used as the children age; the environment may change what it teaches but the school still designs it to be a safe space for students to learn. The problem is that the only thing school focuses on becomes term tests, instead of making sure the students actually understand what they are supposed to.

The elements of Math, Science, History, and Psychology should be applied to the other subjects that are taught in school. These subjects are so broad that their elements are present in most other subjects, (ex: Biochemistry, Archeology, Physics, Anthropology) so these subjects should be given special treatment to make sure the students are given proper groundwork in these fields. Let's take a personal trainer for example: if you want to become one, you need to have a good understanding of sports psychology, so that you can properly collaborate with your clients; but you also need a good understanding of anatomy and metabolism so that your client can optimize their physical body.

One of the hardest challenges that the education system faces is trying to find an effective way to define academic success. Because what can actually be used as a proper measure of your success in high school? If you base the idea of academic success on grades alone, then I couldn't call myself a good student. Despite this, I found myself doing quite well in lots of classes, but because I struggled with the concepts of others it makes me a bad student. The problem with using grades alone is that it doesn't take into account the students' actual behaviour in class, it just bases the student's ability on a collection of random test scores. I found that I did very well in the classes such as art, gym, and linguistics, but struggled more with theoretical classes such as Math, Science, History, and Computer programming. Looking at grades alone, this proves that not all classes are for everybody and that we all have strengths and weaknesses. What schools should do is try to weave different subjects together as they teach, this would allow students to have more practice using concepts like history, psychology, and science in varying ways without forcing them to take a separate course in the subject just to be educated in it.

The question remains, do grades reflect academic success in school? The answer lies in Howard Gardner's nine forms of intelligence, which clearly explain that the ability to perform well in class is not completely based on behaviour but is also based on your natural affinity to specific subjects. Since we all learn things at a different paces, it's unfair to consider two people with the same grades an equal merit if they put various levels of effort into their work. Take me and my girlfriend for example, when we were in school, she would help me with my studies because school was her specialty. From making me flashcards in math, and fixing my grammar in English, to helping me study for my upcoming tests, my girlfriend was the key to my success in later high school. But we knew that at some point the tables would turn, since once we'd be out of school, I would also be there to help her with her social interactions and get her out of her shell. The point is, we're a team, and by accepting our strengths and weaknesses we can help each other succeed within each other's domains.

This same logic applies to tests, and it's why when you fail a test you shouldn't consider yourself a failure but consider that you are trying to improve one of your weaker forms of intelligence. The idea of attaching grades with academic success is an old idea that dates back to the Industrial Age values we discussed early on in *Problem 1*. In those days, mass production was a manual process that required you to be able to repeat things over and over, which was reflected in the grading system. The same thing still applies today, especially in the fields of math, science, and business, which are the classes that are considered to lead you down the modern-day equivalent of successful jobs. But if we change the subject and look at popularity for instance, then I had the upper hand, as that was my specialty. The catch is that being popular can be a double-edged sword in some cases. In the case of my girlfriend, it was often for the reason category, as the friendship existed primarily to serve a purpose.

On the other edge of the sword, I was popular through networking and my extroverted nature. Most of my friendships fell more into the categories of seasons, and lifetime friends, which I made in class, but also through clubs, sports, and parties. I first noticed the differences in popularity when would be together in the hallway, as I would be saying hi to everyone I knew, which wouldn't happen as much for my girlfriend. It showed how my relations with people were strongest when we were out of the classroom when the whole situation was flipped for her. In fact, with the way I used to form my friendships in school, we could use that logic for being a person of influence in our social network. If you have connections with certain people who have certain character traits and we associate those traits with you, when it comes to applying for a job it could work in your favour in terms of reference. My popularity in high school also caused my relationship to quickly become public knowledge, which in turn made her more popular since they connected her with me by being my girlfriend. Everyone was initially surprised by our relationship because my girlfriend and I were from two different social worlds. At the time it also would have seemed out of character on my part, because my previous relationships had been with more popular or social girls.

The problem with school is that it focuses on the wrong things, instead of focusing on the students, the focus is on their future jobs. The system focuses on making sure the students can perform as well as possible on their tests but doesn't take into account the student's way of learning or their interest in the subject. Jay Shetty highlights this problem through dialogue between a teacher and one of her students. The student is protesting the way she is making her students look at their future, by explaining to her that they should be looking for a future that makes them happy instead of successful. This idea reflects the way the education system pushes its students into competitive jobs and punishes the students who want to try something else[59].

The happiness advantage also backs up the idea that students should be encouraged to find a job that they consider fulfilling, as the experiment concludes that seventy-five percent of success in any field is dependent on the happiness of the individual. These findings also connect with the concept of the identity crisis discussed by Marcia in *Problem 4*, as employment that is fulfilling and makes you happy would be a large step towards reaching her description of identity achievement. So, let's put all of this together, if you want to do something in life, it has to come from you since you'll be happier and find more meaning in it. All the evidence says that you'll thrive much better in these conditions, and that benefit will also continue to everyone who the job impacts.

---

[59] YouTube, Jay Shetty, *Don't Forget What Life Is Really About | by Jay Shetty*, January 31st, 2019,

Have you ever heard someone say the classic line, "Stay in school kids"? Well, more importantly, look at the person who is saying it. It's usually either someone who regrets having dropped out when they were younger, or it comes from someone with an extremely high education level and typically says it in the sense of "so you can end up like me." Well, either way, the statement is being said by someone who has ironically been failed by the school system. If the first guy regrets his decision to have dropped out, he had done so at the time because the school never gave him the guidance he needed. The second guy stayed in the school system but was guided by the system into a job that's more focused on making money instead of a job that feels satisfying. These problems return to the ideas of school's Industrial Age values, the only difference is that today's education system focuses on shovelling everyone to college or university because the jobs that are now used to run the economy require higher education. The teachers play hot potato with our lives, they toss us around from class to class, which gives them a diversity of voices that say the same thing *"Do what you're told, and don't question me since I know what's best for you."* This is one of the many ways that they replicate the typical nine-to-five jobs, along with the long days, the annoying superiors, the tasks with deadlines and no excuses for not handing them in on time.

This grasp that school has on its students even continues after classes are over because even when students are supposed to have their rest, they are given homework to keep them busy. There's also the weird logic that school uses when it comes to classes, where a student who struggles with a subject still has to take classes about it even if their understanding won't improve. The problem with this is that the teachers won't help the students who are in this position, which just means that it wastes everyone's time. This is why, making sure teachers understand that each student has an affinity with different forms of intelligence is important. Adjustments are needed for many students to learn at the right pace because simply teaching the whole class through lecturing is why students' learning is inauthentic.

We're being lectured about finding our places in society, about choosing the right career for our future, about equal opportunities in life, even if we all know that's not true. All of these things have one thing in common: to be able to get them, you need to lose something else in the process. Success in school is the same thing, you will fail many times in a subject before you ebbing to improve and succeed, but sadly school doesn't give us the necessary room to do so. For example, I suffered multiple setbacks and failures before I began to realize I was abnormally bad at math. It took lengthy discussions with both my parents and my teachers, before I would get a psychological evaluation to diagnose me with dyscalculia, the inability to understand math. However, that evaluation helped me realize that psychology was actually my calling since the psychologist helped me understand how my brain works. Parents need to listen to their children more effectively when it comes to their education because just taking the time to listen to what they have to say can improve their self-esteem; *"It feels really good when you ask me to teach you about what I'm learning or what I'm good at. You don't have to be awesome at computer programming to let me teach you some cool stuff, for instance. I have to be a beginner constantly. Show me it's OK to stay relaxed and present when you are struggling to learn something."* [60]

Giving your child support in school will help them put more effort into it themselves. They will feel more comfortable asking for help when they need it if you show that you'll be there to provide it. It's important to understand that school starts at home, and the child's development will be deeply impacted by their parent's behaviour. The simple fact of having you help your child with their homework or having them explain to you what they learned in school at the supper table will not only help them remember it but that will show that you care about them and their education.

In *Problem 1* we compare the parenting methods of the Authoritarian parent versus the Authoritative parent, it's pretty obvious which of the two is more effective for the child's confidence. The authoritarian parent believes studying is completely the child's job and pushes the kid to develop their independence by neglecting to help them if they are needing support. On the other hand, the

---

[60] Vail, Rachel. "Top 15 Things Your Middle School Kid Wishes You Knew". *HuffPost*, 2016,

authoritative parent sees studying as a process that needs to be nurtured by the parent so that the child can properly understand how to learn. The authoritative parent develops the child's independence by giving them the tools necessary to learn first and then giving them the room to become independent later on. These parents are both trying to teach their children the same thing, but the outcomes will clearly be quite different. The first child will either struggle in school due to a bad work of discipline or might struggle with failure for fear of angering their parents. On the other hand, the authoritative parent's child will be more prepared to learn when they go to school and will not have as much trouble when they fail, because they will help them improve rather than bash them for it. If your goal is to see your child succeed in school, but you don't want to support them getting there, what makes you think they'll want to climb?

Naturally, it can be difficult to balance the role of both the parent and the teacher, but the reality is they are both necessary for the development of your child. The good news is that it will save you lots of trouble in the future, because if you help them when they are young; they will be able to act more independently as they age. Preparing your kids properly for their future will save them a lifetime of stress, as it will make studying and their future work life easier to manage. It will allow them to make the most out of their time so that they can stop and smell the roses while everyone else just runs right past them. The mission of this book is to target the seven big problems in the education system, by

181

explaining why they are so problematic and giving them solutions. And I think I've found the closest model available so far when it comes to trying to solve these problems.

In the Netherlands, there's a school called *"AGORA Foundation for Special Primary and Secondary Education"*[61]. Their director Rob Houben explains their mission: *"We give children the opportunity to play, because when children are playing with something they get interested. And then you don't have to teach, and you don't have to police them either."* To give you a bit of a run-down of their system, they want to give the space and energy of a monastery with the tools, books, and accessories you could find at a university. It's a place that cultivates creativity within students, who are able to try everything without having to commit to a certain course sequence the students are also supported throughout their studies, but also challenged to see how much they understand all the way through. A typical day starts at 8 am, for the mentors to prepare for their daily routine; and while that's going on, the students get to interact with each other for about thirty minutes to socialize. After that, each student has their own agenda, so that everyone comes with a specific purpose in mind, and it's their job to go towards it. Then after lunch, there is thirty minutes of silence for reading, and the day normally ends at 3 pm, but you could stay longer if you need to do some extra work on your projects.

[61] Agora. Hundred.org. January 10th, 2022,

Problem 1: Old Age Values, is solved by having a mission that promotes creativity, innovation, and a student-centred learning system. This is done by giving them the tools and the space they need to explore on their own, redefining the values of learning and why you send children to school.

Problem 2: No Room for Autonomy, which is solved by having no curriculum because the system is too rigid, and it brings stress to both the teachers and the students. The teachers feel like they are not suited to teach their classes because the curriculum is not up to their standards. But it also brings stress to the students because it shows that their success is based on producing good grades. Since at AGORA, they know that not all students want to learn the same thing, they give them the tools and space to explore on their own which helps promote autonomy. Therefore, by not having a rigid curriculum imposed by policymakers, there's no stress on the teachers or students, and they can focus on planning individual learning plans for each student.

Problem 3: Outdated Learning System, the solution to this problem is solved by removing the idea of a curriculum because the rigid curriculum that's set-in place brings stress to both the teachers and the students. By removing the curriculums, you can take what you want out of a subject, which creates a student-centred learning system. In fact, this makes the curriculum your plan, and the books are whatever you need to succeed according to that plan. Also, to add to the effectiveness of the learning experience, they have guests come in and instruct the students about different things or a student can go to learn about a certain thing that they had planned to learn.

Problem 4: No Room for Passion. This is solved by having a wide variety of subjects a child could choose from and the tools needed to succeed. As much as having too many choices isn't better, it leaves the students who know what they want to do and those who aren't sure they have time to explore. We all want to fight for equality, but we forget that equal opportunity doesn't mean equal outcomes. This is easily shown in the test taken, teachers give an equal opportunity to answer the same twenty questions but not all students answer it correctly, therefore some students pass and some fail. Also, every ninth grader in high school is offered the same six mandatory classes to have an equal opportunity to explore them, however, some might take, and some might not take next year when it becomes an elective. Therefore, instead of promoting equality where everyone no matter what has the same things, they promote equity where everyone is given what they need to succeed.

Problem 5: We All Learn Differently. The solution is that each student should be given the ability to find a way to study that works for them, and they should also be given the tools needed for their specific learning method. In the classic school system, you have a class based on age with a variety of cognitive abilities. At AGORA it's the opposite: not only do they not have any classrooms, but they also encourage kids to work together towards a common goal, no matter the age or cognitive ability. This helps improve communication between students as well as their ability to interact with people from different intellectual backgrounds.

Problem 6: Lecturing, is solved by allowing the students the freedom to learn as they please, but to ensure comprehension by talking about what they've learned with their teacher.

Problem 7: The Inevitable; The Unexpected; The Pandemic, this isn't a direct problem with the education system but with the pandemic brought a semi-permanent switch to it. Because of the pandemic we we're forced to adapt to our changing environment. However, this is something that AGORA has already implemented. Because they know that a vast majority of the students don't have a clear idea of what they want, everything that could be useful to find out is there to help them. Meaning for a student who is exploring their option, it's expected for them to switch and in the process, they find what they don't want, it just narrows the opportunities down.

From the seven problems mentioned in this book, there's one thing that I think englobes all of them; collaboration and understanding that both the parents and the teachers share an equal responsibility in the role of a child's learning. Sadly, parents think all the learning happens at school, and teachers think all the learning happens at home, but only students know that learning happens everywhere. This is why in the AGORA system; you have the parents and the "teachers." And the students all have a role to play in the education system, which has many similarities to the Waldorf approach in education due to the fact that parents or grandparents would come in and help. The reason I think having your parents involved can be important to your academic success is because they could find tools to study for a test and support you while you're doing your homework. And that's all thanks to the parent-student-teacher meeting since you don't even have those in post-secondary school so how could parents and/or teachers judge the student if they don't properly assume their role in the child's academic success?

Simply put, in the AGORA system the class sizes are kept small, with only seventeen children of different abilities being placed together. This system is okay because the students who are more independent are allowed to do their own thing while the others can collaborate with their coaches to set up a personalized curriculum. The coach's job is to make a learning plan that can remain dynamic for the students, this way the students can learn their curriculum at their own pace without the stress of time or deadlines to break their rhythm. Now last but not least, the parents have an especially important role: to volunteer daily with anything when available and drive students to locations that they need to visit for learning purposes. They even have internships for parents to allow them to share their hobbies and make workshops out of it, which also allows students to understand what the nature of their parents' jobs is, and could help them, develop a better idea of what it means to be in the workforce.

With all that being said, would you like to join the **Academic Revolution**?

References

Problem 1: Old-aged Values

YouTube, Visions of Helsinki, Why Finland has the best education system in the world, September 15, 2016,

[2] *TOP 25 QUOTES BY JEAN PIAGET (of 73) | A-Z Quotes*. A-Z Quotes. August 11th, 2022,

[4] Perera, A., & McLeod, S. The Pygmalion Effect. Simplysociology.com. April 6th, 2022,

[5] YouTube, ABC News Australia, "Why Finland's schools outperform most others across the developed world" January 31st, 2020,

[6] CIEB, "How Long Is the Average School Day,"

[7] YouTube, World Innovation Summit for Education (WISE), "homework: Finland does it better" October 25th, 2013,

[8] *How working too much affects your heart*. Sunrise Hospital and Medical Center. February 17th, 2020,

[13] YouTube, TEDx Talks, "TEDx Bloomington - Shawn Achor - "The Happiness Advantage: Linking Positive Brains to Performance" June 30th, 2011,

[4,] YouTube, Jay Shetty, "If work stresses you out, watch this," August 30th, 2019,

[15] *Inspirational Quotes by Rollo May (American Philosopher)*. Inspiration.rightattitudes.com. February 10th, 2022,

[17,18] Mulder, P. March 7th, 2022. *7 38 55 Rules of Communication*. Toolshero.

[19] Vie, C. *Les enfants et l'intimidation*. Noovomoi.ca. August 27[th,] 2012,

[20] "Albert Einstein Quotes About School | A-Z Quotes". *A-Z Quotes*, 2021,

Problem 2: No room for autonomy

[21] YouTube, Next school, "6 problems with our school system", December 15th, 2016

[22] Symes, J. *Waldorf Steiner - Progressive Education*. Progressive Education, February 5th February 2020,

[24,] YouTube, WISE, "What if Finland's Great Teachers Taught in Your Schools?" August 8th, 2014,

25 Thomson, A., Thomson, K., & Houston, A. The Pudding. February 2019. "The Sexualized Messages Dress Codes are Sending to Students."

26 YouTube, Vox, "Teaching in the US vs. the rest of the world", January 11th, 2020,

24,25,26, Freed, Josh, and Jon. Kalina. To Kill or to Cure: Parts 1 & 2. Galafilm Productions, 2002.

Problem 3: Outdated learning system

27 Cunff, A. The forgetting curve: the science of how fast we forget. Ness Labs. April 22nd, 2022,

28 Schacter, D., 2020. Daniel Schacter's Seven Sins of Memory. Exploring your mind. November 28th 2021

29 "Hermann Ebbinghaus." AZQuotes.com. Wind and Fly LTD, 2021. April 6th, 2021.

30 A-Z Quotes. 2021. *Albert Einstein Quote*. June 24th, 2021.

31 *TOP 13 QUOTES BY KURT LEWIN | A-Z Quotes*. A-Z Quotes. August 12th, 2022,

33 Pullkett, T. *How to teach your kid what transgender means*. Today's parenting. June 14th, 2022,

34 YouTube, Escaping the ordinary (BC Marx), "rich dad, poor dad," February 2nd, 2021,

35 A-Z Quotes. 2021. *Jack Kornfield Quotes About Letting Go | A-Z Quotes*. June 16th, 2021.

[36] The Infidelity Recovery Institute. August 29th, 2017. *The Four Types of Intimacy - The Infidelity Recovery Institute.*

[37,38,39] Arcc-cdac.ca. 2005. *Sex Education in Canada.*

[40, 4] Pullkett, T. *How to teach your kid what transgender means.* Today's parenting. June 14th, 2022,

[42] Nolen, Jeannette L. "Bobo doll experiment". Encyclopedia Britannica, May 26[th,] 2020.

[43] *Ontario unveils new science curriculum focused on engineering design, coding | CBC News.* CBC. March 8th, 2022.

[44] Summary: What makes for a high-impact career? 80,000 Hours. April 10th, 2022,

Problem 4: No room for passion

[45,46] YouTube, The Atlantic, *"Why perfect grades don't matter",* November 30th, 2017,

[47] Thomsen, M. *"Get Rid of Grades.* Slate Magazine." June 1st, 2013,

[48] Gruner, E. *"I no longer grade my students' work – and I wish I had stopped sooner."* The Conversation. March 29th, 2022,

[49] Hoque, E. *Stanley Hall "Storm and Stress" Theory-B. Ed Notes*. Educare Centre. July 5th July 2022, from

[50] *Marcia Four Identity Statuses*. January 1st, 2021.

[51,52] Daniel H. Pink | The official site of author Daniel Pink. 2021. *Drive | Daniel H. Pink*. May 27th, 2021.

[53,54] YouTube, JRE clips "Everyone Is Not Equal" February 26th, 2019,

[55] YouTube, Jay Shetty, "The ONLY VIDEO You Need To Find Your TRUE PURPOSE In Life," January 13th, 2021,

Problem 5: We all learn differently

[56] Marenus, M. Simplypsychology.org. June 9th, 2020,

[57] "Bulimia Nervosa". *National Eating Disorders Association*, June 9th, 2021,

[58] "Albert Einstein Quotes About Intelligence | A-Z Quotes". *A-Z Quotes*, 2021,

Problem 6: Lecturing

[59] Top 10 Sal Khan Quotes. Brainy Quote. July 16th, 2022,

[60] Hierck, T. Best TOM HIERCK Quotes - The Cite Site. June 5th, 2022,

[6] YouTube, Jay Shetty, "Before 2020 ends, watch this" December 31st, 2020,

[62] YouTube, Jay Shetty, Don't Forget What Life Is Really About | by Jay Shetty, January 31[st,] 2019,

Solution: New way to revolutionize school

[63] Vail, Rachel. "Top 15 Things Your Middle School Kid Wishes You Knew". *HuffPost*, 2016,

[64] Agora. Hundred.org. January 10th, 2022,